May God bless
you with thoughts
from my journey

♡ Perry Sparks

My Saturday Morning Posts

PENNY ARMSTRONG SPARKS

WESTBOW
PRESS®
A DIVISION OF THOMAS NELSON
& ZONDERVAN

WestBow Press books may be ordered through booksellers or by contacting:

WestBow Press
A Division of Thomas Nelson & Zondervan
1663 Liberty Drive
Bloomington, IN 47403
www.westbowpress.com
1 (866) 928-1240

THE HOLY BIBLE, NEW INTERNATIONAL VERSION®,
NIV® Copyright © 1973, 1978, 1984, 2011 by Biblica, Inc.®
Used by permission. All rights reserved worldwide.

The term "balcony person" used in the March 24th post was taken
from the book Balcony People by Joyce Landorf Heatherley

Cover photo by Nate Sparks

ISBN: 978-1-9736-7090-2 (sc)
ISBN: 978-1-9736-7089-6 (e)

Library of Congress Control Number: 2019910874

Print information available on the last page.

WestBow Press rev. date: 09/09/2019

This book is dedicated to my sweet husband Scott
and to my boys, Nate, Cooper and Brodie.
You three are my forever reminder of your father's legacy.

Preface

Well here goes...I have always loved story-telling. I feel you just connect with people if you can honestly tell your story. I thrive on hearing stories from others...funny ones, hard ones and those "a-ha kinda moments" where you see things clearly. I had thought about writing a few times, but never really committed until my recent life-altering turn of events. On February 19, 2018, Scott, my sweet husband of 26 years, died. He was 51 years old, and we didn't see it coming. He contracted the flu which lowered his immune system and eventually led to the discovery of MRSA/staph in his body. A piece of staph attached to his heart valve, broke off and spread to his brain causing a massive stroke. He came home from a high school basketball game with the flu on February 6th, and thirteen days later he was gone. There is no way we could have predicted the series of events those two weeks would hold. One week after his death, I posted on social media to let people know what happened and to respond to the hundreds of messages, calls, and texts I had received. I began posting every Saturday morning to keep everyone updated on my three boys (Nate, Cooper and Brodie), my circumstances and my heart. I have been raw and vulnerable before my community of friends and family, and they have encouraged me to publish my journey.

I constantly think of David writing the Psalms. He was

so honest about his struggles, holding nothing back for fear of how he would be perceived. This was also a quality of my sweet husband. Scott had been a student pastor, college minister, church planter, pastor and a high school teacher. It didn't matter what platform or situation he was in, he always encouraged people to share their story and to be honest. He believed God created us to need each other, not pull away when we are broken - to let others carry us and then, in turn, carry others. The inspiration for my posts and this book comes from years of hearing Scott say, *"Share Your Story."* Even as I tearfully type these words, I can almost audibly hear him saying it.

As you read my heart, please remember the words on the page were not carefully crafted and edited for grammar. These were my thoughts and feelings saturated with run-on sentences, chasing rabbit moments, and lots of dot-dot-dots. When my fingers touched the phone screen, these unfiltered thoughts never considered sentence structure or paragraph breaks. Simply put, I was sharing my guts with my community. They were **my people** and they did not critique me in my grief. So...if you break out in hives when it doesn't look right on the page, you might want to say a prayer before you begin reading. Remember that a person's heart and story should never be cleaned up for perception's sake, but heard with grace and compassion. So...here goes!

To those who broke the maximum capacity rules in the ICU waiting room - lining the halls to tell Scott goodbye...

To those who sent cards, messages, texts, emails and called letting me know I was not alone in my grief...

To those who stocked my house with everything I would need for the months to come...

To those who brought meals...

To those who shared their personal resources to meet my financial needs...

To those who mowed my lawn...

To those who saw a need and met the need - not waiting for me to express it...

To those who were not afraid of my emotional incontinence...

To those who didn't just encourage me to move forward but walked alongside me each step of the way...

To those who pushed me to turn my posts into a book and worked tirelessly with me to make it happen...

To those who continue to remind me of the impact Scott made...

I remember everything! There are no words in the English language to fully express the breathtaking beauty of the body of Christ...but I have experienced it. I am and will forever be grateful.

My Saturday Morning Posts

Monday, February 26, 2018

I have been silent on social media since my sweet husband's passing. Many are curious about the chain of events so I will summarize the best I can.

On Tuesday, February 6th, Scott came home early from a basketball game where he was keeping the book. He had horrible chills and flu symptoms. From Tuesday to Saturday he had a terrible time but began to look a little better. During this time he began to develop increasing pain in his shoulder and knee. By Sunday it was excruciating. We went to the doctor on Monday, February 12th, and he was puzzled as to why joint pain followed the flu. Labs were run, Scott was given a steroid shot and sent home. We received a call on Tuesday, February 13th, from the doctor saying labs revealed high sediment levels and to go to the ER. Between Tuesday and Friday, Scott was pumped full of antibiotics and had multiple scans, MRI's, and labs done. He was diagnosed with MRSA/staph (bacterial infection in his blood) which was causing the pain in his shoulder and knee. Surgery was done on Friday night. Saturday was painful, but he seemed to feel better.

On Sunday, February 18th, Cooper stayed with his dad a couple of hours so I could run home to shower and pick up a few things. I returned to relieve Cooper around 10:00 p.m. I had only left Scott three times that week, for just a few hours at a time, with one of our boys. He needed help with a lot and wanted only us. Around midnight, we were talking and his words became jumbled. It scared me because he wasn't making sense, so I immediately called the RN for help. He was rushed out of the room. I called Nate who was at my side in minutes. They took us to an ICU waiting room where we waited until 3:00 a.m. and were then told he had a brain bleed. At 5:00 a.m. another scan was done that revealed it was worse. The doctor was kind but honest…"He will probably not come off the ventilator." I turned to Nate and said, "Can you drive?" My strong twenty-one year old son drove home to get his brothers and I made THAT CALL to Scott's parents. When Nate returned with Cooper and Brodie, I explained to them that even if he was not fighting the infection throughout his entire body, their dad had been given only a 3% chance of surviving. I told them that Scott and I had this conversation and I knew what he would want, but I wanted the decision to be all four of us. They all agreed that Dad needed to be given to God. We waited for Scott's parents to arrive to share the events, made him comfortable and removed the breathing tube. In the hours this process took, I saw my children tell their Dad how much they loved him, had learned from him and how they would never forget his lessons. They promised to take care of me, but the most beautiful promise was that this would not shake their faith in God that he had so intentionally instilled in them. We all made that promise!

There was this holy moment where God showed me how much I would see Scott in my boys in the coming days. They have been my rock. Their perspective and raw faith have been a consistent reminder that my husband led well. So many of you came to the hospital, have been in my home, and traveled many miles to be at his funeral. I have begun to read texts, emails, messages and posts. Know that I savor every word. His life was only fifty-one years, but was a beautiful expression of how God calls us to live. My Scott loved his Heavenly Father passionately and that love manifested in how he loved others. So many of you have been generous with your time and resources and with each act I am increasingly humbled. I have seen the body of Christ at work and it is breathtaking. Just know that in my grief

I hold tight to my trust in our Sovereign God. I am not afraid and I do not doubt my loving Father. I am reminded daily to place my dependence on him. I cannot say that one verse or passage of scripture has been my comfort for there are too many to choose from. As I look forward, I am reminded that **SECRET THINGS** belong to the Lord, and the future things are **SECRET THINGS**. Know that I will never be able to express the gratitude I have for your hearts. Please continue to pray for me and the boys as we walk through every detail of our lives.

Sunday, March 4, 2018

Tomorrow is March 5th and would have been Scott's fifty-second birthday. Today the boys and I will celebrate the way he loved to do birthdays. First, a day is picked when we can all be together ALL DAY (because experiences are the best presents). The birthday boy chooses the place to eat and the activity of the day. We all love movies and that is usually the choice. Scott had already told me where he wanted to eat and the movies he wanted to see. The day ends with the traditional Sparks' birthday hat and Rita's chocolate cake. So all of these things are on our list today (pictures to be posted later). When I went to pick up the cake yesterday, the ladies at the bakery had it waiting and gave it to me free. With hugs and tears, we talked about how much Scott loved this chocolate cake and how big a part of our birthday traditions it had become.

This was just another reminder of how my sweet husband engaged with everyone around him. Every part of his life was an opportunity to know people and let people know him. I have had a beautiful, hard, humbling, potent, full, accountable, tearful, sweet kind of week. Daily posts, calls, texts, cards and visits have brought an array of emotions. Having high school and college kids in and out of my house all week has made me feel more normal because that is the way we lived. Scott and I always loved a full house.

On Monday, I began the task of sorting through every detail of our lives and recapping my circumstances with every call. I have felt like someone whose skin is raw and bleeding from pulling a bandaid off over and over again. I would work each day until I could not breathe or could not tell my story again. With each day, I would recall how intentional and prayerful my husband was with every decision that affected our family.

My Monday through Thursday was only seeing those who came to visit or bring food. I got up each day and put on one of his t-shirts and a pair of his socks. I sat at his desk with his pen and computer hoping to make him proud of me. My morning moments were seasoned with holy reminders from God. His words were..."Trust *me*, I love *you*, *you* can do this, talk to *me,* be aware of *my* presence." Then came the big one..."***Live Penny***!"

> *For to me, to live is Christ and to die is gain.*
> Philippians 1:21

God reminded me that this is how my sweet husband lived and it was time for me to *emerge* from the safety of my home and his desk. So Friday was officially **EMERGE DAY**. I went to the bank, funeral home, car wash and Walmart. I even wore makeup and only lost half of it. God kept whispering in my ear, "You got this girl...you are mine and I am right here."

Please continue to pray for me and the boys as we go through all of Scott's personal things. Each sweet memory I recall as I touch, smell or see something...brings an ache of missing. So tomorrow (March 5th - Scott's Birthday) if you have an opportunity, **EAT CHOCOLATE CAKE** and blame it on Scott. Love you my friends! Thank you for continuing to show how amazing the body of Christ can be! (By the way, I have received over one hundred pictures of chocolate cake or people eating chocolate cake!)

Extra Late Night Sunday, March 4, 2018

Today was a day to celebrate Scott Sparks. Tomorrow he would have been fifty-two. We did all the things he wanted to do to celebrate: movie (if you get there early, you get a rail seat), went to get wings (Scott would never clean his hands until he was through eating his wings so he would pick up his drink with the palm of his hands, fingers not touching - demonstrated by Nate and Cooper), and we took a Sparks Selfie (even though we missed his face in our selfie, Cooper still managed to ruin it by making a stupid face). We are ending our night with the birthday hat and Rita's chocolate cake. Scott will be remembered at every special occasion because our family traditions were built around him. We did it up right, My Love!

Saturday, March 10, 2018

S o it is Saturday morning again and it seems to always be a good time to have peaceful moments. Scott loved Saturday mornings with his Bible, a cup of coffee, a Krispy Kreme donut and our back porch (when weather permitted). Always the first one awake, he loved greeting each of us as we entered the living room still waking up. This week has been a mix of emotions with more details that require a death certificate and removing his name from things. With each task, my heart hurts because our names have been side by side on everything for twenty-six years. The boys and I went to pick up everything from his classroom. He was so organized and full of purpose with everything he did, even down to his snack drawer where he would let students partake daily. His neat hand writing had still not been erased from the board, and his stash of supplies for students who just couldn't afford things remained in the cabinet. Those who taught with him said, "Some teachers can teach for years and never have the impact Scott had in six months." I am never surprised by these words, but cling dearly to the reminder that he impacted everyone he met. Still…too much removing this week! The comfort God has given me throughout this has been small reminders that Scott's influence and perspective will never be removed. With every decision and experience, he will be with me.

So many of you continue to call, text, message, bring food, send cards and give generously to me. This week has come with good conversations and hard ones. I have also laughed at all the memories.

I have entered into a new classroom and God's lessons have comforted, inspired, challenged and convicted.

*And we know that in all things God works for the good
of those who love him, who have been called according
to his purpose.*

Romans 8:28

Not all that happens in this life is good, but God will make it
work ***for the good*** and He will get the glory! I will hurt, but
I will trust.

*Therefore he is able to save completely those who come
to God through him, because he always lives to intercede
for them.*

Hebrews 7:25

I am reminded that Jesus intercedes for me. He works ceaselessly
on my behalf. My God not only walks beside me, holding my
hand, but ahead of me. Psalms 139 (the "Search Me" chapter)
tells me that **MY GOD KNOWS ME!**

*Consider it pure joy, my brothers, and sisters, whenever
you face trials of many kinds, because you know that the
testing of your faith produces perseverance.*

James 1:2-3

My days will be full of interruptions that will encourage me to
try to do things on my own. I must choose to walk in humble
dependence even in the small stuff. My weakness equals His
strength!

People keep affirming my faith and strength but it is a pure
manifestation of God's faithfulness in my life. Even when God
totally changes my direction I am reminded to seek first his
kingdom instead of powering through with my plans.

But seek first his kingdom and his righteousness, and all
these things will be given to you as well.
Matthew 6:33

God used Scott to pull back on my reigns for twenty-six years and I will forever remember my husband's ear to the heart of God. That is how he led. I have a heightened sense of my need to slow down and listen.

For to me, to live is Christ and to die is gain.
Philippians 1:21

This has been not only the theme of my sweet husband's life, but a challenge for my every step.

My boys are nothing short of amazing! They still have boy moments and I still have mom moments, but they walk soundly with me through it all. I rejoice in their lack of fear or worry. God will forever forge their paths and I am confident they will walk passionately in the direction He calls them.

Summary: I wake up every morning and say, "I trust you God." I cry every day at some point. I work through daily details with deep breaths, good friends and God's voice. Each day brings more of my "new normal." My hurt comes from the missing. To all of you...I love your guts!

Saturday, March 17, 2018

It is interesting that when you go to post on social media it says, "What's on your mind?" My mind has been everywhere this week. Nate and Cooper both left last Sunday morning for their spring break trips. I was so glad they were going, but I have to admit I had to fight my fears for their safety. God reminded me we are not called to live life safely. A huge part of seeing God work through you is living this adventurous life he has given. I want to always encourage my kids to chase the experiences God has for them. Sometimes, I can measure my energy level against the challenges ahead and think I can't do it. God gave us his Spirit to empower us to live beyond our own strength and ability. He is not limited, therefore I am not limited (lesson one for my week).

I struggled with my reminders this week. There will be a day when they are beautiful memories, but in my tenderness right now, they remind me of Scott's absence: setting all the things we loved to record on the DVR, his old slippers he would not replace because he couldn't find any he liked as much as the ones he already had, the way he would set my coffee cup out on the counter with sugar/creamer/spoon just waiting on me to start my day, the sweatshirts we bought on the day he proposed, his razor in the shower, his Rx sunglasses that he loved because he could still look hip and see, the cards and notes in his drawer he had saved...from me and the boys. My home is so completely full of him...as it should be.

I have also been reminded that I can't just trust...I must hope. God does not want me to live just passing time. My sadness tries to strip me of my hope for the future. God desires me to live in anticipation of what he has next. I have said God wants me to **LIVE,** but this week I see my living will be a *leaning* process. That is not a typo - I meant to say *leaning*, not *learning*. I have shared with some of you that my living has been daily steps. God reminded me this week of the children of Israel in the wilderness. He gave them manna, but just enough for each day. If they tried to store it up, it would ruin. It was a lesson in total dependence. God gives me just what I need to face my day, and I must fight the urge to want a supply saved up. I have a humble need for him every morning. My God is my manna (lesson two).

I am a doer. Moving and accomplishing makes me feel better. The key is...the things I am doing may not be the most important things or the things God desires from my day. My peace and joy comes from walking closely with God. He promises I will rejoice, heal and have joy again. It will not be about what I accomplish, but **WHO HE IS!** I must learn to rest in him (lesson three).

> *Be still, and know that I am God;*
> Psalms 46:10

My dad came back in town on Monday, and he and my mom left on Thursday. It was so good to have Mom with me, but it is time to wade into my "new normal." I have to adjust to the quiet and doing things on my own. I have to make decisions and be responsible for everything. God whispers in my ear..."I delight in you and will be here in the big and small."

> *Ask and it will be given to you; seek and you will find;*
> *knock and the door will be opened to you.*
> Matthew 7:7

The Lord your God is with you, he is mighty to save. He will take great delight in you, he will quiet you with his love, he will rejoice over you with singing.

Zephaniah 3:17

I can do everything through him who gives me strength.

Philippians 4:13

I am keenly aware of my weaknesses, and this keeps me focused on God's steps for me (lesson four). Some of my lessons repeat or overlap, but God knows this repetition is needed.

I had sweet moments with people of all ages this week. You have continued to call, text, message and post. I am confident that you, my friends, will be used powerfully in my healing. I am grateful that we were created to need community and it is unreal how I see my God in each of you. I will return to work on Monday, which is also the one month anniversary of Scott's first day in heaven. Pray that all the lessons I have shared with you will come flooding back in my hard moments.

As always...I love and treasure your friendship.

Saturday, March 24, 2018

S aturday morning seems to be my spot in time for solitary moments of reflection. This was my *first* week back at work, but before Monday morning, I had another *first*. Brodie and I went back to The Grove Church on Sunday morning. Some of you don't know the story, but I promise to be brief. We (Scott, Penny and an amazing team) planted a church a little over eight years ago. Last July, Scott stepped away as lead pastor because God told him it was time to pass the baton. So many people did not understand, but as always, when God told Scott to do something, he was obedient. It was a beautiful transition, not abrupt or shocking. Through the creation of bylaws, development of a leadership team, and the move into a permanent building, God gave Scott peace about passing the baton to Josh Duncan, the current pastor. Earlier in the year, God led Scott to Josh, and over the next four to five month they led together as Scott slowly handed over the leadership of the church. There was nothing but joy in Scott's heart to be faithful to God's desires even when so many just didn't get it. Once again, a beautiful picture of trust in God and not the ways of man.

We decided that Scott needed a job during this time of "what comes next," since we had two kids in college. Two days before school started, he was hired as a high school history teacher (more evidence of God's provision). When I walked into The Grove last Sunday, I was flooded with memories of Scott's heart, his passion for this church to be a light to the community and his love for the people. When you enter the building, you see a long wall with the The Grove Leaf logo and this verse:

When he had finished praying, Jesus left with his disciples and crossed the Kidron Valley. On the other side there was an olive grove, and he and his disciples went into it. Now Judas, who betrayed him, knew the place, because Jesus had often met there with his disciples.

John 18:1-2

The garden, sometimes referred to as the grove, was a place that Jesus often met with his disciples. Scott would say he could imagine them hanging out, laughing, crying, and praying together. They had **CHURCH** in that grove. Many of you may not know this, but God gave Scott that vision about twenty-five years ago when we were newlyweds in seminary. We talked about how amazing it would be and never knew it would happen almost twenty years later. God's plan and timing is perfect. Those of you who have had any part of The Grove Church, please know how strategic God has been with this vision. Scott's legacy is not The Grove Church, but his faithfulness to simply be obedient.

After my Sunday moments came returning to my work family on Monday. I work for a hospice, and I can honestly say, I could not go back to this job right now if it were not for the family I have there. Each sweet personality and the way they love me makes me feel safe and strong at the same time. I'll be honest...I cried a lot this week (not the best when you are attempting make up). But with each of my moments, my co-workers stopped the busyness of their tasks to give me all the time in the world. They also let me be normal and push myself forward. Many of you have heard me refer to being a "balcony person" - that person who stands in your balcony cheering you on. This week, my balcony had an overflow room attached.

Once again, "thank you" and "I appreciate you" seem so

small in expressing how I feel about your calls, texts, posts, messages, meals and hugs. I think I am working on a new word for this...we will see if Webster's Dictionary approves.

My boys continue to be a walking reminder of not only Scott, but his faith invested in them. They love deeply, serve wholeheartedly and strive to see God in not just the present, but the future. Our conversations are precious gifts.

God's whispers in my ear this week:

You are not alone. I am the author of your moments.

> *Do you not know that your body is a temple of the Holy Spirit, who is in you, whom you have received from God? You are not your own;*
>
> I Corinthians 6:19

> *To them God has chosen to make known among the Gentiles the glorious riches of this mystery, which is Christ in you, the hope of glory.*
>
> Colossians 1:27

The painful reminders of Scott's absence will turn into sweet memories...be patient.

Let my spirit remind you of my purpose for you. It's not just about trusting, but hoping for things to come.

> *Now it is God who has made us for this very purpose and has given us the Spirit as a deposit, guaranteeing what is to come.*
>
> II Corinthians 5:5

Remember I am your God who spoke the world into existence and has been your strength. Unlimited power! Let my presence be like a magnet that draws you close to me in your weakness.

> Surely God is my salvation; I will trust and not be afraid. The Lord, the Lord is my strength and my song; he has become my salvation." With joy you will draw water from the wells of salvation.
>
> Isaiah 12:2-3

> Surely you have granted him eternal blessings and made him glad with the joy of your presence.
>
> Psalms 21:6

Thankfulness must temper your thoughts. It is a remedy for your sadness because a grateful heart glorifies me and fills you with joy. I am a consuming fire.

> Therefore, since we are receiving a kingdom that cannot be shaken, let us be thankful, and so worship God acceptably with reverence and awe, for our "God is a consuming fire."
>
> Hebrews 12:28-29

I don't just provide...I give in abundance!

> When they had all had enough to eat, he said to his disciples, "Gather the pieces that are left over. Let nothing be wasted." So they gathered them and filled twelve baskets with the pieces of the five barley loaves left over by those who had eaten.
>
> John 6:12-13

How priceless is your unfailing love! Both high and low among men find refuge in the shadow of your wings. They feast on the abundance of your house; you give them drink from your river of delights. For with you is the fountain of life; in your light we see light.

Psalms 36:7-9

I will never change...even in your changing circumstances.

Jesus Christ is the same yesterday and today and forever.

Hebrews 13:8

For I am the Lord, your God, who takes hold of your right hand and says to you, Do not fear; I will help you.

Isaiah 41:13

Pray that my deep breaths will be followed by an open heart and hands ready to grasp this abundant life I am called to.

Saturday, March 31, 2018

It is already Saturday again. I had just finished posting my heart last Saturday when the doorbell rang. It was my plumber. I had called him about my leaky toilet. I didn't really know him because Scott had primarily been the one who took care of that stuff. Luckily, my sweet husband put how he knew people in the subtitle of his contacts, so I just put in plumber and his name popped up. My problem was not really a problem, but my fear of a problem. I started to tell him why I was so fearful of anything going wrong - because I feel responsible for everything! All my "everything" was shared for twenty-six years and now I feel the weight of it all. Something gave me pause...what if this man doesn't care? What if the most difficult thing I have ever walked through doesn't matter to him? I don't think I could handle it! Then God reminded me to be brave and share my story. God whispered gently in my ear, "Share your story so they are drawn to my story." So I explained to my plumber why I was so paranoid about something breaking. I didn't know if he was a believer or even a compassionate man. I was just taking another page from Scott Sparks' book. When God says do it, ***be faithful!*** When I finished, he shared some of his own loss and how God had given him peace. Before he left, my plumber prayed over me. His prayer included the same verse I had just read in my morning time with God. Scott's life and death will forever be a part of my story. My lesson was of faithfulness and courage. Sometimes God turns scary moments into beautiful blessings.

Sunday was good. Church and dear friendships are comforting. That is what church is supposed to be - a place where we are challenged and renewed to go out into our week and make a difference. The value in the assembling of believers far exceeds our understanding, and that is why scripture tells us not to abandon it. After church, my friend, Mary Beth, walked with me in my next step forward. I went to pick out the newest member of Team Sparks - a puppy. Scott and I had talked about adding a puppy to our lives again, even down to potential names. Not only was this something he would have wanted, but I think I need this now more than ever. My sweet friend has given me the nudges I needed and in the next two weeks, Phoebe will join our crew. As I showed pictures of her to Brodie, I had this moment where God whispered, "I will give you things to be excited about. Take joy in looking forward." My new puppy will be part of my learning to hope. Thank you, Mary Beth, for my gentle nudge... or maybe push.

Thinking about my next few weeks became intensely painful. Easter, Mother's Day and Father's Day, will all take place within two months. We were a party of five the last time we celebrated these holidays. I decided that I would focus on all the celebrations we had experienced and not the ones we would miss having with Scott. I will choose to rejoice in the resurrection this Easter week. Because of God's plan, my sweet husband is in heaven. Because God loves us so much, we are promised so much. The resurrection is yet another example of trusting when we don't understand. Can you see the disciples' devastation and confusion when Jesus was taken from them? I feel it! But then the plan unfolds - the sovereign plan that pieces it all together. So I choose to be thankful... because I do have a choice. I will be thankful! I will have purpose! I will have hope!

Now it is God who has made us for this very purpose and has given us the Spirit as a deposit, guaranteeing what is to come.

II Corinthians 5:5

I say to myself, "The Lord is my portion; therefore I will wait for him."

Lamentations 3:24-26

But those who hope in the Lord will renew their strength. They will soar on wings like eagles; they will run and not grow weary, they will walk and not be faint.

Isaiah 40:31

You make known to me the path of life; you will fill me with joy in your presence, with eternal pleasures at your right hand.

Psalm 16:11

I had a really rough evening this week. I am still continuing to go through Scott's phone and found what I thought was a series of pictures of him. Instead, they were videos, and before I knew it, I was hearing his voice - that voice I had not heard since February 18th late at night in a hospital room. I did the "can't breathe" ugly cry. I miss that voice so much. After I calmed down, I watched them all. They were promos for The Grove's move to a permanent location to be posted on social media last fall. It was fun to watch him attempt to summarize seven-plus-years of a journey into a one minute video. In the videos were some funny bloopers that were peppered with all his mannerisms. It was good to laugh at him and remember him with humor. Later on, my kids and I watched some fun old video footage. Remembering can be healing.

There were times this week I was tempted to skip or skimp on my morning moments with God because of tired eyes or schedules. It is second nature to step back into a hurried pace. When I take time to be still in God's presence, I get the greatest gift - Christ in Me. It needs to NOT be what God can give me, but GOD IN ME!

> *Therefore, I urge you, brothers and sisters, in view of God's mercy, to offer your bodies as a living sacrifice, holy and pleasing to God - this is your true and proper worship.*
>
> Romans 12:1

> *Yet I hold this against you: You have forsaken your first love.*
>
> Revelations 2:4

> *To them God has chosen to make known among the Gentiles the glorious riches of this mystery, which is Christ in you, the hope of glory.*
>
> Colossians 1:27

So, this week I got new glasses. It's interesting that new glasses provide new vision because this week has been about hope, and new vision gives new hope. Even in painful moments, I am beginning to feel hope. For me to see clearly the hope God has for me, I have to be receptive and attentive. It brings a vulnerability and readiness to the table. All of this new vision brings unpredictable peace.

> *You will keep in perfect peace him whose mind is steadfast, because they trust in you.*
>
> Isaiah 26:3

This week also brought time celebrating the birthday of my sweet friend Sandra and time out with a group of ladies. It was good to laugh and celebrate the goodness we experience through friendship.

> *There is a time for everything, and a season for every activity under heaven:*
>
> Ecclesiastes 3:1

My week ended with Brodie's track meet, plans for Easter, ordering graduation announcements for Nate and laundry. All things that are just parts of a week yet they brought joy, hope, perspective and lots of emotion. On Friday morning at 5:45 a.m., I heard the wind chimes out back on the porch. God reminded me that in all my moments, tears, and lessons for the week...He knows me!

> *For I know the plans I have for you," declares the Lord, "plans to prosper you and not to harm you, plans to give you hope and a future. Then you will call on me and come and pray to me, and I will listen to you. You will seek me and find me when you seek me with all your heart. I will be found by you," declares the Lord, "and will bring you back from captivity. I will gather you from all the nations and places where I have banished you," declares the Lord, "and will bring your back to the place from which I carried you into exile.*
>
> Jeremiah 29:11-14

In verse 11, He tells me he knows my future.

In verse 12, He promises he will listen.

In verses 13 and 14, He reminds me I will find Him.

My prayer for all of you this week is Peace.

> *Taste and see that the Lord is good; blessed is the man*
> *who takes refuge in him.*
>
> Psalms 34:8

Happy Easter!!

Saturday, April 7, 2018

My Saturday morning posts had been so easy until today. Now, I have a seven-week old puppy vying for my attention. If words are not spelled correctly or grammar is a little off, please show some grace. I was up with Baby Phoebe at 4:30 a.m. because she decided she had slept enough. She has finally fallen back asleep on my lap, so here goes.

In just the past sixteen hours, God has reminded me of the dependent love I need to have for him. Of course, this involves our new addition. Everyone has dropped in to see this adorable ball of fur, but the reality of her comes with her not knowing anything. She has never been on grass, so potty training has been a challenge. She has only had one successful potty outside and countless failures inside. I have been rushing her to the grass hoping to teach her that this is the place to "do her business," only to have her look up at me with eyes that say, "Sorry…but I think I am starting to get it Momma." The one time she did make it outside, she knew this was the ultimate goal (probably the happy dance I was doing with her).

When I think of my lessons for the week, God's repetitive patience is ever present. I am a gun jumper! I want to plan ahead, be prepared and know what's coming. The thing is... God only reveals in his time. This need I have to power up, conquer or fix all that comes in my day, including my emotions, is not God's way. He daily reminds me that my only prep for the day is practicing his presence. So it is a good, successful and productive day when I am close to God all day long. Just like Phoebe, I had many failures this week, but God patiently waited for me to "do my business." When I had those few moments of victory, I felt him doing the happy dance for me.

...pray continually;
I Thessalonians 5:17

... in all your ways acknowledge him...
Proverbs 3:6

If I can go out of chronological order...my Easter was good. Tears began the day because I missed my sweet preacher husband. He loved Easter because he felt it is one of the few times a year people came through the doors that never "do church." No matter the reason they were there, he loved watching the Holy Spirit do his thing (fresh starts, new beginnings, grace, unconditional love).

This year had a different feel for me. The boys and I drove early Sunday morning to see family in North Carolina and on the way we made a stop at Scott's grave. A variety of thoughts and emotions flooded over me:

Easter in heaven must be unreal.

I am not going to be sad about him not being here this Easter because I am thankful for all the ones we shared before.

God loves us so much he sacrificed his son, and now Scott is living the dream in heaven. Once again, I am thankful.

A thankful heart will be my goal this week. I will need God's peace to have this kind of heart.

Like a gardener God plants his peace in me, but there are these weeds that grow too quickly (let's call them fear, worry, sadness). The peace so gently planted in my heart has to fight to endure these weeds. However, what I gain from the fight is worth it. I have to trust my gardener to kill the weeds as they grow.

> *And my God will meet all your needs according to the riches of his glory in Christ Jesus.*
>
> Philippians 4:19

My God will provide for all my needs... including peace.

Time with family, and even travel time with "da boys," was good. There were God-ordained conversations throughout the day. If I can be honest, the week had some lonely moments not because there was not someone around, but because I felt that no one really understood my heart. God reassured me that in those moments, he is infinitely and abundantly accessible to me. This was yet another nudge to practice the presence of God. My lonely moments disappear in his presence! I am still learning what it means to quiet my heart.

> *He makes me lie down in green pastures, he leads me beside quiet waters, he restores my soul. He guides me in paths of righteousness for his name's sake.*
>
> Psalms 23:2-3

He restores my soul...

> *Now to him who is able to do immeasurably more than all we ask or imagine, according to his power that is at work within us.*
>
> Ephesians 3:20

This also applies to my emotions! I had some good moments with my kids this week (I use the word moments a lot but I like that word). I am THANKFUL for the friendships they have that encourage and push them in their faith. I love hearing what God is doing in them.

I guess my last thought is one from earlier. I want thankfulness to be as natural as breathing for me. I was reminded of the creation story in Genesis. Here stands Eve with this amazing garden before her equipped with everything she would ever need. However, she chose to focus on the one thing God told her she could not have. My heart desire is to not look at what I don't have, but be thankful for all I have been given.

Dear friends...know I am thankful for you!

Saturday, April 14, 2018

Well, there have been many events and lessons this week. Summarizing is not my strength, but I will recap best I can. Let me just start by saying, I forgot how much time a puppy requires! After last Saturday, I was wondering if I heard God wrong about this decision. But as the week progressed, God revealed his purpose and timing; it is daily teachable moments with her. My words to her remind me of the repetition God has in my life.

"No No!"…I am going to stop you there before you do or think something that is not good for you.

"Where are you going?"…I know the plans I have for you - that direction is not part of it.

"Come here sweet girl and let me love on you,"…Slow down and drink in how much I love you, then go out with joy as you face what comes next.

"Do your business,"…Don't be distracted by your surroundings. Focus on the task I have in front of you right now.

Phoebe also went to work with me this week. We are calling her an emotional support/therapy dog. She has about twenty-five extra mommas now. All week long, everyone would pop in and check her out for a dose of puppy love. Her simplicity reminded us all to take deep breaths in our day and have perspective. I literally had someone come in and say, "Rough afternoon…can I just have some Phoebe time for a little bit?" I honestly think we might have all been a little more productive and full of joy with her around this week. God works in furry ways sometimes.

In my busy week with my new puppy, track meets, early mornings, financial decisions and graduation prep for Nate, God reminded me of his perfect analogy...I am clay. Like a master potter molding his creation, each event of my life is part of God's preconceived plan to get me to this point. When I am practicing his presence, it is like his smooth hands are shaping me. Even when he has to work on the rough edges - when there is resistance in me - I feel his purpose. I may not understand it, but I want to trust the Potter's hands.

> *Yet, O Lord, you are our Father. We are the clay, you are the potter; we are all the work of your hand.*
> Isaiah 64:8

> *But blessed is the man who trusts in the Lord, whose confidence is in him.*
> Jeremiah 17:7

I see how easily I can be distracted. Similar to Phoebe, I can have spiritual ADD. I can be content to be resting in God's lap but then a task pulls me away. In that moment, I am the one who walks away; but when I turn back, God is still sitting there waiting on me and rejoices when my thoughts return to him. He is my constant.

> *Jesus Christ is the same yesterday and today and forever.*
> Hebrews 13:8

God's constant presence has reminded me to bring the smallest of requests to him. My treasured time with God in the morning is like nuggets of gold to my day. I wasn't sure Phoebe was going to see it that way, so I asked God to help me maintain this precious time. Now, when I sit down with my coffee, Bible and journal, Phoebe stops what she is doing to lay down beside me. Remember, she is a puppy, so that is totally a God thing!

I had more rough moments this week. I went to one of Brodie's track meets alone. Recently, I had Nate with me as my support, but this time I felt like I was being stared at. When I came to an event alone in the past, people knew it was probably because Scott was with another son at their event. Sometimes, we would tag team and switch off. If they fell on the same night, we would each get in a race and maybe three innings of a baseball game. Either way, we always made sure the boys had at least one loud voice cheering them on. Now when I show up alone, it is because...I *am* alone. I am learning how to be alone, but the fear of what people are thinking creeps in. I don't want to be that person that people avoid because they don't know what to say. I want to be the same loud mom who cheers for their child like they're breaking an Olympic record. So my challenge for this day was to not focus on others actions or thoughts, but simply be the passionately expressive mom I had always been in the past.

A day is meant to be lived within its twenty-four hour boundaries. God knows our human frailties can only handle so much...one day at a time. Once again, his sovereignty is clear. He knows we max out at twenty-four hours. We take on each day separately in total dependence, only looking back to learn and pressing forward to live.

This is the day the Lord has made; Let us rejoice and be glad in it.

Psalms 118:24

Brothers, I do not consider myself yet to have taken hold of it. But one thing I do: Forgetting what is behind and straining toward what is ahead. I press on toward the goal to win the prize for which God has called me heavenward in Christ Jesus.

Philippians 3:13-14

I walked into my closet this week to get ready for bed. I am still adjusting to seeing his clothes and shoes, and even his bedtime routine in my mind's eye. The promised warmer weather for the next day caused me to glance to the far left of the closet where my short-sleeved clothes are kept. There it was...my wedding dress so carefully sealed up in its see-through bag. As I sat in my closet crying, I remembered every detail of that day, especially those beautiful vows that ended with "till death do us part." My twenty-three year old self had no idea that it would only be for twenty-six years. My heart was broken, but once again, God swooped in and reminded me of all that those twenty-six years brought - God's calling to go wherever and do whatever with no boundaries to our trust. We did it the way we said we would. When we stood at that alter, we not only made a vow to each other but to God. We committed to be an unstoppable team for his glory. I have no regrets about the twenty-six years we shared and that feels so good!

Whatever you do, work at it with all your heart, as working for the Lord, not for man,

Colossians 3:23

My need for movement seems to be magnified because slow moments bring on "missing" tears. I want so badly to have an agenda so I don't have to think. Sometimes, thinking needs to be on my agenda, but sometimes God wants me to have quiet days where nothing happens. He says, "Use this time to seek my face." When he gives me no special guidance or task, maybe I need to stay where I am. **Sitting still is not wasting time!** One thing that has come from this lesson is patience. In the past, my life was so scheduled and planned. Things not on the schedule could easily be viewed as interruptions, but now I see them as opportunities. This has been the result of practicing God's presence - seeing God in the small stuff.

Today I was reminded that heaven is not just my future, but my present too. Holding on so tightly to God's hand gives me a taste of heaven now. I am thinking that being near to God is going to be the best part of heaven. We get glimpses of heaven now as long as we slow down and are attentive.

My last words might have been a good stopping place, but I told you I struggle with brevity. Last night Phoebe and I were taking a late night trip to the front yard to "do her business" when IT happened. For a little background to the story, there is a wreath on my front door. I am not a wreath person, but this was one from the funeral and it was beautiful with spring flowers, so I decided to put it on the front door for a while. I remembered quickly after why I don't put flowery wreaths on the door - birds make nests in them. I had a few friends and the UPS man dodging the birds so I decided to check it out. There was a nest but no eggs, so I felt ok removing the nest. They would go somewhere else…right? Well, apparently they *were* attached to the arrangement on my red door because there was another nest built there this week. Last night when I opened the door, they flew at us. I think this probably hurried Phoebe's potty process along. We were celebrating her achievements in the yard and heading inside not knowing the bird had returned to the nest/wreath. When I opened the door, I guess it was seen as an invitation because my bird friend came on in. Well, you can imagine the screaming that went on. This was followed by, "What do I do?" thoughts, and Brodie tearing down the steps ready to attack a home invader. Phoebe was carefully tossed to Brodie while I ran for the broom to gently assist our late night guest with her departure. Brodie was saying, "What do we do?" as I vigorously demonstrated what we were going to do. After much chasing and broom swinging, our friend left through the front door. I cleaned up the feathers and stress-induced bird poop, then held my puppy who probably has PTSD now. Brodie and I had to laugh at the events of the past hour. We took the wreath down and it is still lying in the flower bed right now. I am sure every bird for miles knows not to mess with the "red front door house." When these moments come, I think how hard Scott would have laughed about it and he would have been proud to see me choose fight over flight (no pun intended).

May you pull close and see God in all the small moments this week.

Saturday, April 21, 2018

If I had to use one word to summarize my week, it would be CHOICE! In this beautiful relationship I have with my God, he has given me a choice. He really sacrificed to give us this freedom - to let us make our own decisions. When everything else about us is under control, our actions or our tongue, the mind can still rebel. The mind is like the last fort to surrender. When all of me (my mind included) is practicing God's presence, I find peace. Genesis 1:26-27 says we are made in God's image. God gave us a choice. It was **HIS** choice to give **US** a choice. He knows how beautiful it can be when we decide on him and his ways.

. This week I had to choose to let God take hold of my thoughts. My go-to thought has been, "May my life be punctuated with thanksgiving." The core of my gratitude is God's sovereignty. My perspective is limited, and even though he gives me glimpses of the *why*, it is better for me to decide "just because" I trust him.

> *For we live by faith, not by sight.*
> II Corinthians 5:7

> *give thanks in all circumstances…*
> I Thessalonians 5:18

Lots of decisions this week and even small ones can overwhelm me. Do I purchase this? Is that a wise investment? Every decision feels big and permanent...etched in stone. I have paralysis from analysis. I am so used to having another opinion. When my mind tries to figure it out by itself, I am reminded that I have the ultimate financial consultant just waiting for me to ask. And, **HE** comes highly recommended.

> *Do not be anxious about anything...*
> Philippians 4:6

I knew this week would bring some sadness because it marked two months since Scott's death. Halfway through the week it came out of nowhere. I was training new hospice volunteers and our topic for that session was "Bereavement and Anticipatory Grief." I found myself teaching from my own experience. My own freshly forged path was coming out of my mouth. I felt myself about to burst into the ugly cry, but I knew that would cause them to lose focus. I prayed with everything in me, "God help me keep it together till the end." When the last one left my office, I shut the door and immediately thanked God for his provision. Sandra looked at me and said, "How did you do that?" Well, needless to say the ugly cry followed.

I later remembered a friend in college who told me she thought I was "tough and tender." She went on to explain that was a compliment because Jesus was "tough and tender" as well. I kept coming back to that comment. I believe that when someone is tough, it doesn't mean they are mindless and hard - quite the opposite. It means they know their limitations but have a confidence that says, "Forget rational - I can do this. Even when it doesn't add up, I will do this." It's a confident commitment! As far as tender goes, I do feel tender right now. Not uncontrollable emotions like weeks ago...but tender, like a deep bruise. People can see your physical bruises, but emotional ones are harder to identify. However, when bruises are barely touched, it causes you pain. *I am tender!* But the wonderful thing about bruises - they heal. Even though sometimes it takes time, they eventually become something you remember, but with less pain. The thing is...I would rather be tender than hard. When something hard is dropped, it shatters, unable to be restored or mended. So once again, I choose to be "tough and tender." My confidence is in my God, not my abilities. My tenderness brings the promise of healing, not shattering.

On this same day, I went by the cemetery to confirm the final design for Scott's headstone. I was reminded that decisions are important, but not always etched in stone. Scott's headstone will read, *"For to me, to live is Christ and to die is gain. Philippians 1:21,"*...now ***that*** is permanent!

My refuge during this hard week was rest. Sleep did help with my emotional exhaustion, but the ***rest*** I am referring to is ***rest in God.*** When painful things call out for my attention, I ***rest***...right there in the moment.

During one of my difficult days, I took a trip to Hobby Lobby on the way home from work because I had to replace the bird drama wreath from last week. As I strolled down all the aisles that shelved quotes/verses creatively written on distressed wood, I realized this was probably not a wise decision. Verses and sayings about home, family and love are all things that looked different for me right now. Then there it was, simply written on a canvas, "It is well with my soul!" This old hymn written by a man who had just lost everything was the very song I sang in Scott's ear in the hospital room. I wanted him to know that I would be ok. Needless to say, I was tender all over that aisle in Hobby Lobby. When I am attentive, God shows up and ministers to my heart in ways that human words and touch fall short. His power is made known in my weakness.

> *They will have no fear of bad news; his heart is steadfast, trusting in the Lord.*
>
> Psalms 112:7

So do not fear, for I am with you; do not be dismayed,
for I am your God. I will strengthen you and help you; I
will uphold you with my righteous right hand.

Isaiah 41:10

My thoughts this week have also been about our younger years. We were so "young, dumb, and broke," to quote a new pop artist, Khalid. I am watching my kids learning to manage their time, money and making decisions. There are some things you don't learn from Mom or Dad, but learn from simple life experience. As my boys navigate these waters, the one thing that gives me peace is God's presence in their lives too.

Nate (22) will graduate in three weeks. I am so proud of him, but also just excited for his next adventure. I love how he looks for what God has next with passion, anticipation and NO FEAR! This week, Cooper (19) was chosen to be a Young Life Leader at Karns High School next year. This is the very school where Scott taught his last six months. The mission of this ministry is building relationships with high school students with the purpose of leading them to walk with Jesus. He sent a text the other day asking me to pray for him because he was going to the baseball game to hang out and meet kids. He was nervous. I told him this was his thing. For my people-oriented son, building relationships comes as easily as breathing. I can't wait to see God work in this new experience. Cooper is also preparing to work at a Young Life Camp in Arizona for the month of June. I just feel God's hands all over his new season of life. Brodie (16) is my there every day, protective, make me laugh boy right now. He has always been my cautious child, never jumping without surveying, but now forced into this unpredictable, and at times, very uncomfortable world. I have to say, he is grabbing hold with both hands. Phrases like: "What do we do," "Let's take a look at it," and "I got this," keep coming out of his mouth. God has given him courage and confidence. It is so fun to watch this develop in him. My cup runneth over...

The bottom line for my week, has been God's unfailing love and presence. Doesn't matter if I am "tough or tender," his feelings for me are unwavering and unconditional. His care for me is not dependent on my performance for the day. My CHOICE is to be thankful and delight in his unfailing love.

> *The Lord appeared to us in the past, saying: "I have loved you with an everlasting love; I have drawn you with loving-kindness..."*
>
> Jeremiah 31:3

> *I delight greatly in the Lord; my soul rejoices in my God. For he has clothed me with garments of salvation and arrayed me in a robe of his righteousness, as a bridegroom adorns his head like a priest, and as a bride adorns herself with her jewels.*
>
> Isaiah 61:10

> *Let your face shine on your servant; save me in your unfailing love.*
>
> Psalms 31:16

> *Let them give thanks to the Lord for his unfailing love and his wonderful deeds for men,*
>
> Psalms 107:8

Saturday, April 28 2018

This morning, I woke up just automatically thinking of my Saturday morning post. It has been a huge part of looking back over my week to see God's hand in my life. I have to be honest...I asked God if I was supposed to write this morning. So much of what I have learned about myself this week revolves around my comfort in planning and routine. Let's face it - don't we all feel more confident if we know what's coming? A quote by Sarah Young hit home; "A mind preoccupied with planning pays homage to the idol of control." Stopping to ask God about his plans for my day keeps me practicing his presence. It is so easy to assume that if something is productive and good, it's a God thing. Waiting on God with confident trust is an active and passive thing. When I learn to sit still with God, this quietly builds trust between us. When the rough stuff hits, I am actively participating by trusting God and not being afraid. My fear manifests itself with excessive planning. I read this week that when problems come that have no quick solutions, I have a choice to go up or stay down. The down option is looking at things from the "where I am" point of view. The up option is to see my problem like a ladder that helps me climb up to see things from God's point of view. Here is the 2-for-1; this perspective comes with his presence.

> *Many are the plans in a man's heart, but it is the Lord's purpose that prevails.*
>
> Proverbs 19:21

> *My sheep listen to my voice; I know them, and they follow me.*
>
> John 10:27

All this "changing the way I think" stuff requires FOCUS. Another word picture from my week is a ballerina spinning around and around. She must keep returning her eyes to a specific point to keep her balance. I love that! With everything whirling around me I have to focus (fix my eyes) and return to that focal point where God refreshes my perspective.

For my eyes are fixed on you, Sovereign Lord...
                                        Psalms 141:8

Let us fix our eyes on Jesus, the author and perfecter of our faith, who for the joy set before him endured the cross, scorning its shame, and sat down at the right hand of the throne of God.
                                        Hebrews 12:2

You have made known to me the path of life; you will fill me with joy in your presence, with eternal pleasures at your right hand.
                                        Psalms 16:11

My heart felt split this week. We celebrated Nate's 22nd birthday. It is difficult not having Scott with us, but I want those times to be about celebrating and not missing. Can you feel both and do it justice? I don't want every milestone, event or celebration to bring a lump in my throat from holding back my tears. I decided the one thing that helps is to simply say "Your dad would have loved this." It keeps him with us minus the sadness.

Part of my week has involved re-watching and first-time watching Marvel movies (because the new Avengers movie came out this week). I am a mother of boys and it would be easy to say I was forced into it. Not true! I LOVE super hero movies. There, I said it. I love the way the hero or heroine just does the impossible.

> *He gives strength to the weary and increases the power of the weak. Even youths grow tired and weary, and young men stumble and fall; but those who hope in the Lord will renew their strength. They will soar on wings like eagles; they will run and not grow weary, they will walk and not be faint.*
>
> Isaiah 40:29-31

I have gained encouragement from this verse over the past few weeks, but one part I feel lacking is the ***soaring***. I used to have such an adventurous heart (like Wonder Woman) - never seeking danger or an adrenaline rush, but not afraid of a challenge. I feel overly cautious and careful right now...not afraid...just careful. I want that part of me back.

This week involved last minute detail in the planning of our Volunteer Appreciation Lunch for Hospice. Every year has a different theme that makes it so much fun to plan. This year it was an Oscars motif..."And the award goes to..." There was gold, silver and black everywhere, a popcorn bar, movie candy, fancy finger foods, a red carpet and napkins folded like envelopes placed strategically on gold charger plates. Phoebe also wore an evening gown. So much fun! It was a reminder of one of the things that brings me joy - loving and celebrating people!

This week God has used my kids, my friends and my job to paint this picture of his overwhelming presence in my life. May his creative and strategic brush strokes bring him all the glory.

Saturday, May 5, 2018

This morning I opened my social media and there was that little pop up where it showed my posts in the month of April. There was a family picture of us, along with other pics, then a caption scrolled across the screen; "You did April Right." Kinda funny...how would they know that? As I moved from April (my doing it right month...LOL) to May this week, I experienced three things: crying...whispering...scratching. I know that sounds random, and honestly, I could even add the word "random;" but God has been immersed in all I have walked through, so I lost any belief in random a long time ago.

Last weekend was very emotional. I could not stop crying on Saturday/Sunday. I had a few possible explanations, but my body felt like it had no option other than a hard cry (you know, the kind of cry that makes every part of your body tense.) It infected my days. Miscommunication with Cooper led to thoughts of him being gone for a month this summer. Preparation for Nate's graduation caused me to take inventory of all the things Scott and I talked about needing to share with Nate. Watching Brodie come and go throughout the weekend while my tears confined me to the house showed me how easily depression could creep up on me. I just missed my Scott. I missed his arms around me telling me it would be ok. I missed not having to explain how I felt because he just understood me better than I did myself. I know in my head that God gave me a tangible gift of himself in Scott. I know all the verses that comfort, strengthen, and empower me...but I just felt broken and unrepairable. I read *James 1:2 - Consider it pure joy, my brothers, whenever you face trials of many kinds.* My words to God were, "This is not a trial...it's a devastation." Then the verse came...

But he said to me, "My grace is sufficient for you, for my power is made perfect in weakness." Therefore I will boast all the more gladly about my weaknesses, so that Christ's power may rest in me.

II Corinthians 12:9

So right now I am boasting in my weakness. People kept affirming my strength and I needed them to know...I am broken, I am weak, I am needy, I cry daily. But in the end... Christ's power lives in me.

To top off my tearful weekend, I was told my friend Dwayne Sanders went to be with Jesus on Sunday night. He had been battling cancer for four to five years. Dwayne was fifty-one (like Scott), married to Lisa who is forty-nine (like me), married twenty-seven years (one year more than us), with a daughter Nate's age, and a son Cooper's age and committed his life to the ministry in his twenties (like Scott)...I could go on. Their deaths were different because Dwayne knew it could be coming and Scott's was unexpected. But the key thing was they lived life not promised tomorrow, but with victory in death. I don't believe one kind of death is harder or better than the other. The preparation for your last breath is encompassed in all the moments you lived before. Dwayne was my fellow camp counselor, van driver and mission trip adventurer. His heart was full of Jesus and that manifested itself in a desire to see students come to Jesus.

With my tears this week came a restlessness. My devotion one day this week said when this happens to whisper God's name. I decided to try this out. When people distractions happened I cried out, "God!" When I wanted to burst out in frustration or worry, I cried out, "God!" My attempt to live intimately connected to God's presence was not easy at first, but then it began to be like returning to something that more than comforted me...it restored me. I want to live in awareness of him moment by moment. My whispers were frequent this week. If anyone asked if I was talking to them, I would just say, "No, talking to God." They can't call you crazy for that.

> *"Who of you by worrying can add a single hour to his life..."*
>
> Luke 12:25-34

Had an "a-ha moment" while alone this week in my office. Scott had just purchased a few things for his classroom this semester. He was so excited about his refrigerator, microwave, coffee pot, fan and stool. They all have stories for a later time. I decided to move some of these items to my office partly for function and partly to have him close during my day. In the process of moving things around, I picked up my Holly Hobby lunch box. I had it on the corner of my desk. This was a present Scott and the boys had given to me a few years back. He had researched it on Ebay and found the one I had in 1st grade down to the matching thermos. I had told many stories about this lunch box. That was just how he rolled - my Scott was thoughtful about gifts. He never gave flowers on expected holidays, but on the days I didn't see them coming. He rarely gave me roses...but loved showing up with red gerbera daisies, because he knew I loved that they were happy flowers. He paid attention to the details in my stories and was keenly aware of all my favorites. He knew the "why" behind all the things that made me smile. I just sat at my desk and cried...again. I will miss our love language (acts of thoughtfulness). In this moment, God whispered back, "Let me love you in these moments. You are just scratching the surface. My love for you is BIG!"

...to grasp how wide and long and high and deep is the love of Christ.

Ephesians 3:16-18

When I look at my week to come, I can so easily shrivel with thoughts of details and emotions surrounding Nate's graduation. I want to drink in my God's power, strength, peace and goodness. This is part of grasping the wide/long/high/deep of God.

So to summarize this week...I cried really hard, I did a lot of whispering to God and I began to scratch the surface of what it means to know God. I am intrigued by all the things he can do in me with just seven days.

Saturday, May 12, 2018

It's Saturday morning and I am up early to just have "my time" with God. Nate's graduation is this afternoon and even with the excitement/chaos of the day about to hit, I am feeling calm. This week, God gave me this amazing warm-up to the race I am about to run. Once again, proof that there is no "it just so happens" or "as luck would have it…" My God knows me and my "go-to" habits.

Saturday was all about getting the outside of the house cleaned up for family coming in. Pressure washing, cleaning porch furniture - basically removing the layer of yellow pollen from everything. While watching the boys, I was reminded of these days with Scott. He would get them up early and work till it was done, no attitude tolerated. The funny thing was hearing them say, "Ok, watch me - what would dad say to me right now?" They remember everything...they may laugh about it now, BUT THEY REMEMBER!

I thank my God every time I remember you.
Philippians 1:3

As my week began, I carefully orchestrated my mental checklist that rapidly became a written list of all that needed to be done before family got here Friday. I needed to gain control of my week. I don't know why I associate control with security. Focusing on the tangible is easy because it is right in front of me...calling out to me. It pulls at me to focus on the urgent instead of the important (not a new lesson for me, but a constant chink in my armor). It's interesting...the thing that makes me feel secure is the very thing that makes me vulnerable.

So *we fix our eyes not on what is seen, but on what is unseen. For what is seen is temporary, but what is unseen is eternal.*

II Corinthians 4:18

So I am relaxing in sovereignty this week. I know I will be attacked with details, memories and unexpected turns, but God promises so much in these moments and **He** does not disappoint. With every alteration to my so-called plan, he has stepped in and shown me **His** perspective on things. I will trust my teacher, my friend, MY GOD (shout out to Lauren Daigle for her song, *Trust In You*)!

And we know that in all things God works for the good of those who love him, who have been called according to his purpose.

Romans 8:28

You intended to harm me, but God intended it for good to accomplish what is now being done, the saving of many lives.

Genesis 50:20

...always giving thanks to God the Father for everything, in the name of our Lord Jesus Christ.

Ephesians 5:20

Saturday, May 19, 2018

It is not only Saturday morning, but exactly three months since Scott left for a better place. I thought last weekend would be hard with Nate's graduation and Mother's Day, but it was beautiful in many ways. Today seems to be unpredictably mixed with thoughts and feelings. Graduation was such a sweet time. Nate wore Scott's college ring to have something of his dad's with him. He looked so grown up and so much like Scott. As busy as I predicted the day would be, it seemed to be much more relaxed than I had anticipated.

I have heard the words, "I am blessed beyond measure," but never really knew what they meant till last weekend. "Beyond measure" means - enormous, huge, gigantic, countless, immense, indescribable, inexpressible, mammoth, and hidden. Interesting that the word "hidden" is included in this list. I think sometimes our amazing blessings are hidden from us until just the right moment. Mother's Day followed and my heart was full of the gift Scott had given me and will continue to give through my boys. Once again, I am "blessed beyond measure." Their gifts and our day together were both perfect...just like Scott would have planned. They know the things I appreciate and enjoy: good food, girly presents and a super hero movie. They have me figured out.

> *Humble yourselves, therefore, under God's mighty hand, that he may lift you up in due time. Cast all your anxiety on him because he cares for you.*
>
> I Peter 5:6-7

...give thanks in all circumstances, for this is God's will for you in Christ Jesus.

I Thessalonians 5:18

Thankfulness seems to be a frequent theme for me, but also has taken on a whole new meaning. I am thankful for God's ways even when I don't understand them. I am thankful for an opportunity to learn in my sorrow. I am thankful for my boys. I am thankful for a God who knows me and loves me "beyond measure."

I thought that this week would be more relaxed compared to the days before. "Thought" is the key word in that sentence. I was faced with Cooper's car breaking down in Morristown, tow trucks, AAA, mechanics, frustration with my ignorance in the world of cars, fear of being taken advantage of and desire to be wise and full of grace. You know what???? *Luke 1:37 says, "For nothing is impossible with God."* This is not just a cool saying to paint on barn wood for a decoration. It's a promise.

I will only share one part of the story for time's sake. The mechanic in Morristown fixed what he thought was the problem and the next day Cooper drove it back the hour distance to Knoxville only to break down again two exits from home. More tow trucks, AAA, and financial decisions hit me in the face just hours before the boys and I were headed to Atlanta for a Braves game. I stopped in the moment and asked for that unending supply of wisdom and grace God promised me. He told me not to act in frustration or anger but to allow him to show me his way. So I did. We took care of the immediate and headed to Atlanta to enjoy one of the last times we would have together before Nate and Brodie headed to camp and Cooper headed to Arizona for a month. On the way to the game, I received a text from the Morristown mechanic who "stood behind his work" and wanted to refund my money for the job he did. He explained until he fixed the radiator, the source of the problem probably couldn't be found. No matter what, he wanted me to accept the money back. After talking to the Knoxville mechanic, he was right. I went on to tell my story to the Morristown mechanic. I shared my fear of making unwise decisions and how my husband always took care of car stuff. I told him I prayed for God to give me wisdom and grace. His answer was, "I hope this helps, and if you are ever in Morristown and need anything, I am here."

In the past, my first response would have been anger and frustration because I paid for something to be fixed and it wasn't. God slowed me down and gave me patience and grace, along with an opportunity to share my story with two mechanics. I have to stay connected to the unlimited source I have in God's presence. God is not careless or random with my days. He will equip me for anything if I let him. I have as much of a God as I have faith to receive.

And my God will meet all your needs according to his glorious riches in Christ Jesus.
Philippians 4:19

We live by faith, not by sight.
II Corinthians 5:7

For he said to me, "My grace is sufficient for you, for my power is made perfect in weakness ". Therefore I will boast all the more gladly about my weakness, so that Christ's power may rest in me.
II Corinthians 12:9

Even with my wonderful car lesson, I had some hard moments this week. I think the lack of sleep may have contributed to my heightened emotions, but bottom line...I CRIED HARD! It wasn't a sad, tears rolling down your face cry; it was a wail! I don't think I have done that since Scott died. I was alone, the house was quiet and I was beyond sad. I was sad that every time I now say "the four of us," it is replacing "the five of us." I am sad that I have to make big decisions without Scott. I am sad that going to the grocery store reminds me that I don't buy Scott's items. I am sad because its summer and he loved summer. I am sad for a lot of reasons, and I just needed to scream and wail about it and not scare my kids or make anyone think I should be committed. When my moment was over, I wasn't tired, but actually felt good. God reminded me that his love for me is unconditional and unfailing...not based on my performance. This love is an eternal transaction. I have to lay down my performance anxiety and just let him be God during the good, the bad and the ugly

I want to continue to let all of you know how I am doing (the main reason I started posting every Saturday). But...I also want to encourage you with my honesty. I am not a carefully orchestrated social media poster who portrays herself as she wants others to see her. I want you to celebrate with me in my victories, but also see my failures. I would say "Penny in the Raw,"...but that sounds bad so how about we go with, "What you see is what you get!" Thank you for letting me share my heart and encouraging me to continue to do it.

I decided a few weeks ago to write a letter to Nate with all the things Scott and I wanted to share with him on this special day. I am so grateful that we had these conversations months ago. God knew I would need to know Scott's thoughts and feelings on this day so I could share them. I remember May of 1996, because we were navigating the waters of having a newborn. One of my favorite memories of Scott was how he would stretch out on the couch with Nate on his chest sleeping. He would kiss his head and pray over him while he slept. I see this picture in my heart today. He prayed for Nate to be strong and courageous. He prayed for us to have wisdom to teach him how to love God and love others. He prayed for protection against the arrows the enemy would throw at him. He prayed for the woman who would someday walk alongside him...that God would prepare her as well. These are just a few of the many prayers I heard, but my favorite was, "God, may he be a man after your heart. May he pursue you with everything in him." You can see how writing this letter was not hard. From the first weeks of Nate's life I knew what Scott wanted for him.

I have told you these things so that you will have peace...
John 16:33

For I am the Lord your God, who takes hold of your right hand and says to you, do not fear, I will help you.
Isaiah 41:13

I can do all things through Christ who gives me strength.
Philippians 4:13

Do not be anxious about anything...
Philippians 4:6

Peace I leave with you; my peace I give you...
John 14:27

My days this week felt less like "carry me" moments and more like "walk with me" moments. My week, and specifically today, is like something flavored with salted caramel. The term bittersweet is overused so I am using salted caramel (a flavor I love on and in anything). Every milestone in my life will be peppered with the thought of, "I wish Scott was here." However, I don't think it will take the flavor and sweetness of the moment away. It will compliment every experience. I will savor all the emotions in me and allow this God ordained flavor to bring joy out of sorrow, peace out of pain, love out of longing. So today will be one of many Salted Caramel Days!

Thank you, dear friends, for all of your calls, texts and prayers for my week and today. I am surrounded by such sweetness, and I do not take that lightly. Much Love to you all!

Saturday, May 26, 2018

Today will be my first Saturday morning back porch post. This is where Scott would have been today. This is the first Saturday after school is out and it was a little cooler due to the evening rain. I am sitting here with my coffee cup, Bible and a smile. Lots of birds are enjoying the morning, along with the occasional woodpecker. Everything is CHANGING! Honestly, I have not done well with the thought of change this week. No matter how fun and calm summer may be, it brings another season without Scott. I am reminded of how much he loved living in a place where you so evidently saw the change of all four seasons. Summer means people outside more (and smiling), open-toed shoes, short sleeves and sun-kissed skin. All of it screams things will be different for a while. The world around me has subtly and boldly spoken of change all week. I have had moments where I've been very low. I wanted to sit still and the world demanded movement...change. How could it all keep going without him? I know it's not rational...just a grieving heart. I was reminded that seasons change, my circumstances change...BUT, my God never will. The only comfort to this world's unending change is God's unending presence in it.

I am the Alpha and Omega, the First and the Last, the Beginning and the End.

Revelations 22:13

I have told you these things, so that in me you may have peace. In this world you will have trouble. But take heart! I have overcome the world.

John 16:33

Another struggle this week was "restlessness." I remember when my kids were toddlers they would skip a nap or have a long, tiring day then have trouble sleeping. Made no sense to me - of all times not to sleep...when your body is screaming, "I am tired. Lay down. Sleep!" But I kinda get it now. My emotions, thoughts and anxiousness make me so tired; and when I try to sleep they don't go away...hence "restlessness." I am tired of being tired! I am tired of everything taking so much energy! So...I decided to take naps this week. Just short ones, not sleeps. I have been afraid to nap because I don't want to be awake at night with too many thoughts. So far it has gone quite well - not waiting until I am past my breaking point before attempting rest. Just a "lil somethin' somethin'" to get me to the end of the day. God has been in those restoration moments and he reminds me that I don't have to wait for my breaking point to call out. Saturating my day with "somethin' somethin'" moments has made a difference in my week. God is in prayer. God is in scripture. God is in relationships. But...God is also in naps! There is no formula that says God works only through these specific things. He permeates my every moment when I let him.

> **Be strong and courageous**. *Do not be afraid or terrified because of them, for the Lord your God goes with you; he will never leave you nor forsake you.*
> Deuteronomy 31:6

> **Be still and know** *that I am God...*
> Psalms 46:10

> **Yet I am always with you**; *you hold me by my right hand.*
> Psalms 73:23

What, then, shall we say in response to this? *If*
God is for us, who can be against us?

Romans 8:31

With all the car issues (Nate and Cooper) I had the last two weeks, I have been reminded that God gives hidden treasures in life. Sometimes they are unexpected sweet moments with one of my boys or trials and decisions with cars. They require a little extra work to find them, but they are there. It's not that God is wanting to keep it from us; the lessons are more in the searching and discovering.

> *My purpose is that they may be encouraged in heart and*
> *united in love, so that they may have the full riches of*
> *complete understanding, in order that they may know the*
> *mystery of God, namely, Christ, in whom are hidden all*
> *the treasures of wisdom and knowledge.*

Colossians 2:2-3

It is so easy to allow my mind to jump from problem to problem or even memory to memory, tying my thoughts into this impossible knot! God yearns to help, but he will not violate my freedom. He stands quietly in the background just waiting for me to remember...He is there. I am still learning to walk away from MY PROBLEM and walk toward HIS PRESENCE.

I will come full circle with the topic of change. Phoebe, my new puppy is fourteen weeks. She used to sit still next to me in the morning while I had my time with God, read my Bible and journaled. With age comes less sleeping, more activity and lots of chewing. She has been a blessing...even in frustrating puppy moments. Now our morning time consists of her chewing on the leather strap that binds my journal with an occasional paw on my page...just checking in. It reminds me that sometimes those trials and changes can be difficult but they can also be hidden treasures...soaked in puppy slobber, but still a treasure.

Saturday, June 2, 2018

What a week! Excuse my all over the place post today, but there have been a multitude of things going on in my head. Hard to organize it all, so I'm just throwing it out there for you to sift through. My thoughts are like a rollercoaster - not the simple ups and downs, but all the other stuff: the knot in your stomach anticipating what's to come, the courage to get on the ride and commit to whatever sharp turns are ahead, and the moments that take your breath away. Finally...that feeling that screams, "I did it!"

May ended with me watching Brodie and Nate get on a bus headed to Sharptop (a Young Life camp in Georgia) on Sunday morning then spending four days with Cooper before putting him on a plane. He will be serving at Lost Canyon (a Young Life camp in Arizona) for the month of June. Last post, I shared my struggle with change. Well…nothing like lots of something to help you get off the struggle bus. The first step in facing all this has been honesty. I got up each morning this week and was just honest with God and people each day.

My devotion one day this week was about seeking God in the morning like getting up and putting on clothes. I think back over the past three months and my time with God has been the most consistent thing in my life. It has been not only what makes my day possible, but what pushes me to see God in everything. I put Him on. I see His perspective. I think His thoughts. I used to think my time with God helped me handle whatever my day brought, but now...I see it's not the day that brings my circumstances; it's God. Who better to prepare me for my day than the one who orchestrated it for me! So as I clothe myself with Christ in the morning, I am reminded to walk in grace, humility, patience and wisdom. I stopped apologizing for my weakness because it is the very thing that holds me close to God. I feel like David when he was writing the Psalms. He was so raw at the beginning of his songs/prayers - just threw his guts out there for everyone. But you also see him bring it back around at the end of each one. He talks of strength, faith and dependence when you anticipate him ending his thoughts with abandonment and despair. His wrap up is always his immense love for God. David rode the struggle bus too! He not only got off the bus, but he journaled about the ride.

> *My heart says to you, "Seek his face!" Your face, Lord, I will seek.*
>
> Psalms 27:8

> *Come near to God and he will come near to you...*
>
> James 4:8

> *For in him we live and move and have our being...*
>
> Acts 17:28

I feel God pushing me to let go of my routine. I am afraid if I don't get up early enough to sit still, drink coffee, journal, read my Bible, journal again, my day will be lost. The absence of my perfect combination to begin my day will throw everything off. God has reminded me that the long list of things I have been feeling and thinking, simply put...ARE NOT ME. My grief is not who I am! I have said that over and over this week. It resonates with me.

My four days alone with Cooper were so good. Scott and I always tried to make an intentional effort to spend time with our kids individually. As much as we loved time as a family, there are some conversations that require the one-on-one moments. I was reminded this week of how much Cooper is like me. It's funny that the things that can frustrate me about him are the things that frustrate me about myself...LOL. As I listened to him talk, I remembered being his age and all I discovered about myself and God thirty years ago.

My last three-plus months have been about the highs and the lows, the trials and the blessings, and God's sovereign presence on the rollercoaster that has been my life. But just like that rollercoaster, there are these smooth, calm, straight stretches of life "in the middle" of the ups and downs that also call us to notice God is with us. So as I sat this week and listened to my blonde-haired blue-eyed boy talk about the movie we had just seen, or order food that only the two of us liked to eat...I thanked God for the lessons "in the middle!" - My grief is not who I am!

> ... and they will call him Immanuel which means God
> with us.
>
> Matthew 1:23

On Thursday morning, I was up at 2:00 a.m. because Cooper needed to be at the airport by 4:30 a.m. All of those expected feelings were there. This is the longest he has ever been away from home, and I don't know why I thought it would be easier. Maybe because Nate broke the ice with his month at camp after his freshman year. Then there was Nate's summer long video internship with Malibu, a Young Life camp in Canada (on an island with only a satellite phone). Nate has always paved the way for Cooper's adventures...taking the edge off a little. Well it's different this time. As I saw him walk through security, I realized it was the beginning of the end of an era. When he returns, I will have him at home for a few weeks before he moves into a house with five guys. Things will never really look the same. There will be this new season of independence and that season began the moment he departed on that plane.

The difference between Nate's season of growth and Cooper's was I had Scott holding my hand through it all. As I drove away from the airport, I thought of what he would say…"Penny, this is what we have worked toward all these years. God gave us this amazing child and he called us to equip him to be a godly man. His love for God and others along with this independence is what we desired for him since the day he was born." My heart smiled through the tears because Cooper was doing the very thing Scott and I had prayed for him. He was being faithful and growing into the man God has called him to be.

Thursday kept going with an early meeting at work. My body pushed forward until about 12:30 p.m. then the exhaustion from lack of sleep and emotions sent me home early. I have received so many calls, texts and "check on me" conversation in the last 48 hours. I want everyone to know I am ok. Phoebe and I have been ok with the quiet, believe it or not. We did have help from take-out food, Netflix and some long naps. God's peace hovered over me like a helicopter searching for a place to land. When I got still and threw out the flares, he landed on my heart.

Now May the Lord of Peace himself give you Peace at all times in every way. The Lord be with all of you.
II Thessalonians 3:16

It is June. Nate and Brodie will return from camp today. As I enter this new season, I think of all the milestones I have had and the many more to come. My days will be full of messy imperfection. But the thought of this being part of my journey helps me welcome the rollercoaster moments as well as the "in the middle" moments. Even as I sit here while Phoebe chews on the leather strip that binds my journal, I am reminded that as long as I take a deep breath and feel God's presence with me, like air entering my lungs, I will be ok with my messy imperfection. It is a part of his ways in me.

> *As for God, his way is perfect; the word of the Lord is*
> *flawless. He is a shield for all who take refuge in him.*
> Psalms 18:30

I really liked this verse so I went back to read the entire chapter of *Psalms 18* to see what was going on with David when he wrote this. I discovered he is celebrating how God delivered him from his enemies. He is in huge party mode with God. Found two more verses I held tightly:

vs 19 - He brought me out into a spacious place; he rescued me because *HE DELIGHTED IN ME!*

vs 29 - With your help I can advance against the troop; with my God I *can scale a wall.*

Go David! *(honest, faithful, inspiring)* Praying for a scale the wall kinda week.

Saturday, June 9, 2018

When I opened my journal early this morning to recap my week, I took a moment to stare at it to remember something I wrote halfway through the week. I really love my journal...*it's me.* The pages are soft, but they are bound tightly and hold together even though they are so fragile. I like the way the soft leather makes me feel tender when I open it, calling me to be honest. There are no scripture verses or captions on the outside, no flowers or embossed designs...just worn leather. It's chewed on (thanks to Phoebe), heavy at times, full of my emotions, but still going strong. It is a picture of me and my time with God. How I feel right now - "tough and tender."

My time with God last week kept pulling me to scripture about fear and worry. My mind wanted to ask, "Why?"...I didn't think I felt that way, or did I? Sometimes my emotions circle like an animal seeking entrance. I must remember that trust and thankfulness must be allowed to stand guard.

Summer is here and the past few days brought a typical week. No preparation for a holiday, graduation, camp, or sending a son off for a month - just a plain ole week. So with this came grocery shopping. This is where the animals attacked my safe circle. I found myself in Walmart watching families together loading their carts full of "the family size" of everything. Just a few months ago, I was shopping for four-plus. Nate doesn't live at home but would show up occasionally, so I was prepared. Now it is just me and Brodie at home - a picture of what things will look like in August. No more buying two gallons of milk at a time or "the family size" of anything. I am now just buying enough for two and an occasional extra teenage boy in my house. I remember seasons of thirteen gallons of milk per month. This trip to Walmart was that opening the animals used to sneak into my circle of trust. I am calling these predators **Worry, Fear and Anger**. So how do you close the gap they create? The answer…with what I know to be true!

My emotions took me to horrible places this week. You can know something so securely in your head, but then your emotions bring irrational thoughts. This is why my faith does not rest in how I feel, but what I know to be true.

My emotions said…

You don't have it in you to handle Father's Day.

You will mess up this raising a teenage boy alone thing.

You can't figure out all the complex things you need to know about your family's finances.

Everyone's life just keeps moving without Scott…doesn't that make you mad?

You will never have the energy you need to do it all so just give up now.

So, here are my crossroads…that is how I <u>FEEL</u>…but this is what I <u>KNOW</u> to be TRUE!

> *Consider it pure joy, my brothers, whenever you face trials of many kinds... because you know…*
> James 1:2-5

> *I can do everything through him who gives me strength.*
> Philippians 4:13

You will keep in PERFECT PEACE him whose mind is steadfast, because he trusts in You.

Isaiah 26:3

Delight yourself in the Lord and he will give you the desires of your heart.

Psalms 37:4

Look At the Lord and his strength; Seek his face always.

Psalms 105:4

Lillies of the field...Birds of the air.... Seek first His kingdom.

Luke 12:22-31

(The Do Not Worry Passage)

I have told you these things so that in me you may have peace. In this world you will have trouble. But take heart! I have overcome the world.

John 16:33

This verse in John doesn't say I might, could or possibly have trouble...it says I WILL have trouble...**but God is bigger!**

So this week I learned that when my head and my emotions just won't sync up, I have to trust what is true. What is true brings me back to a grateful heart focused on my God who has perfect perspective.

Thank you God for my Nate who helps me walk through moments with Brodie.

Thank you God for friends and family who tirelessly pursue me.

Thank you for your promises...you ALWAYS keep them.

Thank you for your unfailing word.

Thank you for the life you have given me.

I am looking at my journal now and I see a multitude of thoughts, emotions, lessons, and wisdom all bound up in this "tough and tender" thing. I don't mind being just like it!

Saturday, June 16, 2018

This week was about walking. When I say walking I mean "walking." Not fast mall walking for exercise - just walking. One thing I discovered was how badly out of shape I am. On Tuesday, it will be four months, and I have not done anything truly physical. My emotions have drained every ounce of energy. This can be a vicious cycle because one thing my emotions need right now is some therapeutic physical exertion. The thing about me and exercise is my expectations. I think I should still be able to do all the things I did in my twenty's at the same pace. However, the more I thought about it, I realized that this was not just my approach to exercise but life in general. The key is...those were things God put in front of me for that time. I guess you could say they were along my path. **MY PATH** - no one else's path - **MY PATH.** This is God's uniquely designed route, just for me, with carefully crafted experiences all along the way. No one walks this path but me. Some others may share similar characteristics or moments, but my path is a thumbprint with no duplicate. This means me and my path are God's original, hand-crafted, one-of-a-kind design and with this design there is purpose.

For we are God's workmanship, created in Christ Jesus to do good works, which God prepared in advance for us to do.

Ephesians 2:10

So my path took me to the "battle for my mind." After such a rough week, I decided to change some things. I need a new couch and possibly a chair. That sounds so small, but changing anything from the way it was with Scott takes so much energy. I experience the ole "paralysis by analysis." In the past, there were so many things that I would just pray about and move forward. So, a simple step like just going to shop seemed like a good start. Last Sunday, Brodie and I loaded up and headed to the furniture store where they had a sale going on (cause that always makes you feel better about a purchase). Brodie absolutely hates to shop (but absolutely loves to have an opinion) so I convinced him that, since it was our two rear ends that would be making the most frequent imprints in the couch, he needed to go. After a multitude of questions from him about how long it would take and how many stores we would go to, he settled in, turned on the radio, and resigned himself to furniture shopping with Mom. Then another curve in my path appeared. The dashboard lit up with the battery symbol (and a few other symbols), the radio went off and on, the car sputtered and we barely made it to Nate's house, which happened to be close. Brodie called Nate who was almost there, so while we waited, I decide to pull out the owner's manual. I knew how to charge a battery, but this was different. I came to the educated guess that it was the "battery charging mechanism," and it was going to be a AAA tow to the mechanic. Funny thing... Nate's roommate, Cody, said, "Sounds like your alternator." I responded (with my manual education), "It says when this happens it's the battery charging mechanism." Cody very kindly smiled at me and I responded, "That's my alternator isn't it?" Sweet gracious boy.

In the tow truck waiting period, I went inside and watched a room full of college guys play a video game. I was hot, frustrated and concerned. I had already spent a large amount of money on three of our four cars in the last five weeks. These are all just things that happen when you have cars with over 100,000 miles on them. I kept telling myself it was better than a car payment. Just like the video battle I was watching on the screen, my mind gains things to help me, just to be quickly shot at and wounded again. The "battle for my mind" is fierce, and so many things make me vulnerable to the enemy.

My take away from shopping with a sixteen year old boy/ alternator/video game experience was...I will not despise my weakness. My weakness makes me teachable and what these teachable moment brought me was another opportunity to trust and let God's peace replace the "battle for my mind."

> *The mind of sinful man is death, but the mind controlled*
> *by the spirit is life and peace.*
>
> Romans 8:6

Another realization on my path this week was my "Constant Choice Points" - how many times a day my path is determined by my decisions. I will get through my day no matter what I do, but how I choose to "do my day" can make a huge difference. It transforms my trials into blessings and lessons.

> *Consider it PURE JOY, my brothers, whenever you face*
> *trials of many kinds...*
>
> James 1:2

In all honesty, I did tell God I had enough "pure joy" for the week. LOL...God understands my humor.

My path went all over the place this week with lessons I will share another day, but the biggest take away from this week was my hiking partner. Each day I wake and securely tie the laces of my boots to prepare myself for this one of a kind path I am on. Looking up and seeing God is waiting to take this path with me gives me all I need.

This week's thankful moments:

Hearing Cooper's voice tell me all he is doing and learning.

Hard talks with Brodie that turned into huge blessings in our relationship.

Sweet middle of the night texts from Nate. Exact words my heart needed to hear.

Lunches, dinners and a walk with friends that really get me.

Feelings of accomplishment after so many trials.

Extra sleep and good mental health.

Lessons on pace.

Saturday, June 23, 2018

So here I am again...sitting with my journal, Bible and a cup of coffee. A new addition to all my necessities is a Krispy Kreme donut. Scott would love that I am indulging and got a dozen for $1. I have to admit that writing this post every Saturday has been such a gift. It started as a way to inform everyone of how I am doing because I just couldn't keep up with returning all the texts and messages. But now, it calls me to stop, turn around and look at my footprints from the past week. The entire month of June has been full of unpredictables: feelings I didn't see coming, decisions, parenting moments and a ton of trying new things. So here goes, but I am warning you ahead of time, my thoughts are not brief this week...LOL - I guess they never are.

June 14th was the official day we moved to Knoxville fourteen years ago. I don't know why but dates stick with me. I associate dates on the calendar with even the smallest of memories. With each increase of the year, I stop and look back. I am drawn to looking back even more than usual right now. Father's Day called me to more looking back. I wanted to use the day to support my kids, talk about Scott and laugh hard like he would - all great plans, but it just didn't happen that way. I felt a little like I was a disappointment. In these thoughts, I realized how much I have attempted to do everything the way Scott would have or the way we would have done it together. Decisions, conversations, and plans all have that pressure placed on them. God, in his gentle way, showed me that I have to let go. I need to hold tight to Scott's wisdom, perspective and voice in my life, but, bottom line...I will not always do things the way we would do it if he was here. Circumstances have changed and I have to trust God and do the best I can...WITH EVERYTHING!

Another footprint of my week was Tuesday, June 19th. Four months ago, I handed Scott off to God. The 19th of every month will make me take a deep breath for now...and that's ok. The day was actually really good. My sweet friend Sandra and I laughed about many things that day. I realized that I had been standing on this firm foundation God had given me, but my posture was all wrong. I had my feet dug in, fists clinched, intensely determined to be grounded in what I knew to be true. God has called me to dance - to move about freely on the foundation of His presence with no fear of getting too close to the edge or falling off. The need to be in control or do things just right keeps me stiff in the center with no joy in my journey. When I let go of the need to do everything the way Scott would do it and allow God to guide me, I can relax and even dance. God has IMMEASURABLY MORE planned for me.

> *Now to him who is able to do immeasurably more than all we ask or imagine, according to his power that is at work within us, to him be glory in the church and in Christ Jesus throughout all generations, forever and ever, Amen!*
>
> Ephesians 3:20

My foundation is so secure I can dance on it. My prayer this week was, "God take my controlling intensity and turn it into a dance in your glorious presence." If Scott were here during this "a-ha moment," he would have danced with me!

Conversations with Cooper (via long distance) this week reminded me of a quote I have used endlessly with high school and college students. "Stop trying so hard to seek the answers and seek the ANSWERER!" I heard that in college, and thirty years later, it still has the same impact on me. I can't remember if I read it in a book or someone said it to me, but I know it stops me in my tracks every time I think of it. Nowhere in scripture does it tell us to seek the answers to our questions...it says to seek God. This requires not only quiet moments, but an open heart. God doesn't always tell us what we want to hear...but always what is best for us. Honestly, this takes the pressure off because it asks for my persistence not perfection.

> *You will seek me and find me when you seek me with all your heart.*
>
> Jeremiah 29:13

I realized how much time messes with me this week. It is so hard not to be constantly aware of it. I have THIS MUCH TIME until...I have to get up at THIS TIME to have ENOUGH TIME to get ready for... Realizing that God dwells in timelessness (He was, is, and always will be) means he should be setting my pace. Time with God helps me set my pace according to his design for me. Once again...takes the pressure off. It always seems to come back to seeking God!

> *"I am the Alpha and Omega", says the Lord God, who is and who was, and who is to come, the Almighty.*
>
> Revelation 1:8

My last thought of the week was writing. So many of you have encouraged my grammatically challenged self to write a blog or a devotional book or just a book. I want to say thank you! God and I are still in conversation about this, but it has made me think. So much of my time in the last four months has been guided by devotional books. My thoughts may move on from the chapter topics, but they were my jumping off point. I realized that it's a lot of pressure to be someone's starting point or even inspiration. However, God is the one who uses others words to inspire us, otherwise they are just thoughts on a page. Who knows what will speak to someone? There is no perfect arrangement of the human language that moves us apart from our creator. Once again...pressure removed. If I do write, I have created a new word for it - DEVINSPIRATION! Devotion to my God + Divine teachable moments + Inspiration to live this amazing life He gives. Webster's Dictionary may turn its nose up at my mashup of words, but I think it has a nice ring to it.

Thank you for taking the time to read my run on of thoughts. My posts have never been about the comments, likes or reactions...just sharing my journey and allowing God to use it for His glory.

Love your guts!

Saturday, June 30, 2018

This week had a specific word attached to it - GOOD! Over the past four months, I have been asked a thousand times,…"How are you?" or "How are you doing?" I have tried to be honest and transparent with every reply. My answers have been:

"I'm ok."

"Had a rough day."

"Have had some rough moments this week but doing better."

"Learning a lot about myself."

"Trusting my God."

"I'm tired."

"A lot on my mind and it's hard, but making my way through it."

You get the picture. At times, I may say that certain moments were good or that time with my boys was good, but never…*I'm good.* I have struggled with saying that - "I'm good." Life without Scott could never be good! But this week's lesson snuck up on me. It was a turning point in my heart.

When something takes on the definition of good, it doesn't always mean it feels good, looks good or even tastes good. Exercise is good for you but doesn't always feel good. Medicine is good for you but doesn't always taste good. You get where I am going with this? I had so many good things happening this week. Cooper came home from Arizona on Wednesday. My sister came into town for the weekend. I accomplished some tasks around the house that had been waiting on me. I have a lot to get excited about...but I also had difficult tasks. The "a-ha moment" was realizing that they were ALL GOOD. I began to feel good for the first time in over four months. I discovered that all of the moments in my week were meant for my GOOD. God's ways are mysterious and scripture tells us over and over again to STOP TRYING TO FIGURE HIM OUT...just experience Him.

> *Taste and see that the Lord is good; blessed is the man who takes refuge in him.*
>
> Psalms 34:8

I love the idea of tasting. I always think of Brodie, my picky eater. When he isn't sure he wants to eat what we are pressuring him to try, he approaches it from all angles. He examines how large the bite is and may cut it in half. Then he smells it because that might make it an immediate "NO!" Next is the touching the tip of his tongue to it for a soft taste. Then, after much convincing, he takes it in. It is a perfect picture of how I approach God. I may not like the look, feel or size of something he has placed before me, but I can trust it is good. God has been patient with my need to approach everything from all angles because He knows that once I get a soft taste of his goodness, I will want more. In the past, I might have described my weeks as having the good, the bad and the ugly in them. Now, I am trying to see it all as good...even when it has a kick to it.

Another element to recognizing God's goodness has been my constant awareness of His presence. When Scott died, I woke every morning with my first thought being, "HELP ME GOD!" It was a desperate vulnerability and need for my God. I want to keep that desperate need for my God's immediate presence. I want to open my eyes and realize he does not sleep. He greets me every morning with the promise that he has the day all figured out. Just being able to get out of bed and know my gait is steady - I will not fall because my God walks with me. Now that is GOOD!

So do not fear for I am with you; do not be dismayed, for I am your God. I will strengthen you and help you; I will hold you with my righteous right hand.

Isaiah 41:10

The Lord your God is with you, he is mighty to save. He will take great delight in you, he will quiet you with his love, he will rejoice over you with singing.

Zephaniah 3:17

Let the morning bring me word of your unfailing love, for I have put my trust in you. Show me the way I should go, for to you I lift up my soul.

Psalms 143:8

With the GOOD comes the need to focus on the now - not looking behind me or ahead of me, but focusing on the NOW. It's like trying to walk Phoebe...key word being "trying." She wants to run ahead as far as her leash will take her...to the point of choking herself (not good). But then, she decides she might have missed something in her haste and wants to go behind and backtrack, picking up things she shouldn't. I simply say, "Leave it," and when that doesn't work, I have to manually remove what she's holding in her mouth. But, in those moments when she decides to walk alongside me, it is sweet harmony. I see her glancing over to make sure I am there, then she walks confidently forward. I am my puppy. My too-far-ahead moments choke me. My picking up and holding on to things from my past causes God to constantly say, "Leave it." But, when I walk side by side with him and we glance over at each other, it is sweet harmony.

So, for those who want to know how I am doing - my heart still aches daily for my loss. I still have much on my plate. But...I AM GOOD! Or as Brodie and I say, "It's all good in the hood."

Thank you friends for being a big part of the goodness.

Saturday, July 7, 2018

Every Saturday, I still get the same chuckle when I open up my page to post and it says, "What's on your mind?" From Saturday to Saturday so much happens with me right now. The more I think about it, I hope that never changes. I want God to constantly be working in my heart. I want new lessons and convictions daily. The umbrella word that covered everything this week was COMMUNITY! Scott and I were always passionate about that word. We felt this was where you really saw the biblical version of the church. God created us to need each other. Verse after verse the Bible talks about why God placed us together, how we are called to serve each other, how we resolve conflict with each other...etc. God meant for us to "do life together." This is why you always heard my sweet husband inserting this in sermons and conversations. Small group Bible study was our passion. We were never happier than sitting in a group of people sharing our hearts, honest struggles, digging into scripture to hear everyone's perspective of what they read and praying for each other. This is what the first church looked like. The church is supposed to be COMMUNITY!

> *Therefore confess your sins to each other and pray for each other so that you may be healed. The prayer of a righteous man is powerful and effective.*
>
> James 5:16

> *As iron sharpens iron, so one man sharpens another.*
> Proverbs 27:17

There are so many more verses, but chewing on these for a while might be good.

This is where I see church and community:

Friends who live in my neighborhood to friends who live seven time zones away continuing to check on me and pray when God places me on their heart. Texts, messages, calls, letters that don't require or expect a response... just verses of encouragement or specific prayers for me and the boys.

People going out of their way to answer my questions or help me find the answers, pointing me to people who can help. Sometimes doing all the research for me to save me a step.

People generously providing for me with their own resources with no expectations attached.

People doing things around my house to simply take one more thing off my plate. Not asking if I need it... just doing it.

People inviting me to be a part of any event, group or outing they are going on and not making me feel like a tag-along.

People letting me cry when I need to and also making me laugh really hard and not feel guilty about having joy again.

People being brave enough to challenge me and even call me on my sinful nature.

My list goes on, but these are fresh from this week. All these people are not just my friends, they are my community, my church and the Body of Christ. God created us to need each other. It's in our DNA. So this week, I hope you see an opportunity to be the Community/Church/Body of Christ. Look for it and find joy in it, but also allow others to be that for you.

I will put my pulpit back in my pocket to tell you what I have learned this week. It is so easy to get overwhelmed with all the things I don't know. Brodie and I worked on our grill two weekends ago. This meant sanding off the rust and watching possibly important parts of it fall off with the rust, then repainting it to look presentable on the outside. We were getting it ready to grill last weekend when my sister Kelly came into town. Kelly was going to assist with this education - I never learned to grill. I let that be Scott's thing because I knew if I learned to do it, I would have to do it. So now, it is on the new skill list along with fixing the garage door, maintenance on the treadmill and adding fuel injection cleaner to my car. You laugh, but owner's manuals, YouTube and Google are a default in my brain now. The thing is...through all the emotions, tasks and uncharted territory, my God has to daily remind me that I will never be in control or know it all. The one absolute in my life is my God.

My devotion one day took me to the idea of striving to **know God more** instead of **knowing more**. It talked about knowing God in greater depth and breadth. I have always skimmed over the word "breadth," but with my newfound desire to know things I went to Webster's. The definition for breadth is - the extent of something, freedom from restraint. Think about that...to know THE EXTENT of God with no restraint. This is something that you could strive for and never attain - but what a goal! Part of this striving is knowing he will always be doing something new in me. So the idea of always learning new skills and gaining new knowledge isn't overwhelming anymore. It is part of the breadth (the extent of... with no restraint) of this life with my God.

> *See, I am doing a new thing! Now it springs up; do you not perceive it? I am making a way in the desert and streams in the wasteland.*
>
> Isaiah 43:19

Community and **Breadth** seem to be what I was supposed to share this week. Hope you are encouraged to know others and know God in a new way. Thank you all for being my friend, my community, my church and the Body of Christ.

Saturday, July 14, 2018

Summer only has a few more weeks but for me it is time for vacation. When Scott died, several people told me not to leave town to escape because all I had to deal with and do would still be here waiting when I returned. I would only be escaping my reality. I couldn't have left if I wanted to back then, but now...so ready to leave. This upcoming Thursday will be the five month marker.

The boys and I are about to head to the beach. Scott loved the beach! Some of his comments were:

"My heart rate just slows down when I can hear the waves."

"Don't you think there is a church at the beach that needs a pastor?"

"Seafood just tastes better at the beach."

I loved hearing those same comments every time we went. Because he loved those trips so much, he would make extensive planning lists - what to pack, groceries to take, groceries to buy when we got there, restaurants to eat at with address and how many stars next to their names. Scott had a playlist for every trip we took, and the beach playlist was always growing. He had already started one for this summer's trip. All this attention to detail was because he wanted our experiences together to be amazing. We have so many wonderful memories at the beach as a family.

We never separated from each other except for occasional walks of solitude in the sand. Our evenings were games, cards, putt-putt and movies. We soaked in all this together time. I never heard my kids say, "I'm bored."

We are going back to the coast of Alabama and Florida this summer because that is where we have so many memories with Scott. When we were serving at Calvary Baptist Church in Tuscaloosa, this sweet older couple (Lamar and Louise Hubbs) would give us their beach house free for a week every summer. The name of the house was Hubbward. It was an eclectic mix of furniture with an array of 70's colors (harvest gold, avocado, burnt orange). Every time an appliance would die, a new modern white one would show up in its place and kinda look out of place. There was a closet at the end of the hallway with board games, beach chairs, floats and huge beach hats. Sifting through this every summer was always fun. Our memories date back to when it was just Nate. The summer I was pregnant with Cooper, Nate and Scott dug me a hole so I could lay out on my stomach to get sun. Nate's barely two year old self was very proud of Momma's hole in the sand. A few years back, a hurricane took out Hubbward, but when we go down there, we know exactly where it used to stand.

In my preparations this week, I found all of Scott's beach lists on his computer. I chuckled at the detail, but printed off the list and began to remember. The remembering led to some really rough thoughts. This is my first vacation in over twenty-six years without him. The road trips, tag team driving, packing and unloading...everything moving forward will be memories made with four instead of five. We always knew our crew would grow in the future with daughters-in-law, but I never dreamed our vacation feet picture would only have four sets of sunburnt toes. These thoughts dragged me back down again. I was so disappointed with myself because I wanted to have joy about the trip. This is what he wanted this summer and where we had so many memories of him.

God's voice can be muffled like white noise when it gets

mixed with my thoughts. Sunday night and all day Monday I could not stop crying. I began to beg God to quiet my mind! I prayed for God to give me his thoughts. It's amazing that we can do that. My God and creator gives me the ability to quiet my mind and think his thoughts. It is like being reprogrammed. But it's not a "one and done" kind of thing. It has to be done several times a day. When I feel myself moving back into thoughts of sadness, I have to ask God to give me his thoughts of joy. I want to be thankful I have such sweet memories and not sad that Scott isn't making more with us. So, several times a day this week I whispered, "God help me, take captive my thoughts, give me your thoughts."

> *Do not conform any longer to the pattern of this world,*
> *but be transformed by the renewing of your mind. Then*
> *you will be able to test and approve what God's will*
> *is - his good, pleasing and perfect will.*
>
> Romans 12:2

The main reason Scott loved the beach was because that is where he surrendered his life to Christ. He was a seventeen year old boy walking on the beach when he began his amazing journey with God. I am taking a moment this week to dig my toes deeply into the sand and thank God for that encounter.

My prayer for this week is to be able to remember with joy and to relax in God's presence. Something I read challenged me to lay down my performance pressures so I don't take them into the sacred space of communion God and I share. When I am with a good friend, I relax. I don't worry about what they're thinking. I trust them with myself. I don't feel like I have to be a certain way with God. He knows me down to my core. But relaxing with him like a friend? I forget the friend attributes of God so often. It feels too casual compared to all the other attributes of God. But if we could figure it all out, where would we be? I don't want a God that my finite mind can "figure out." I want to see my God so BIG that I can't get my head around it. I am forever the student learning more about him. So, I am still learning to marry the thoughts of infinite creator and closest friend.

> *Greater love has no man than this, that he lays his life down for his friends. You are my friends if you do what I command. I no longer call you servants, because a servant does not know his masters business. Instead, I have called you friends, for everything I have learned from my Father, I have made known to you.*
>
> John 15:13-15

As I enter my time of relaxation and reflection this week, I will be reminded that there are two sets of footprints in the sand and at times, just one. But those moments are when I am being carried by my friend...You know the story.

Be transformed by the renewing of my mind and walk intimately with my friend...not bad goals for the week.

Sunday, July 22, 2018

I think it is appropriate that my Saturday morning post turned into my Sunday morning post this week. I realized that as of last week, I have done twenty-one Saturday morning posts since Scott died. I not only felt the expectations from others to post yesterday, but also had that expectation of myself. It is interesting that my whole week was about relaxing and walking away from expectations and routine - it was sleeping late, no decisions (except where to go eat), unplanned moments and good seafood. I am such a creature of habit, but aren't we all? We like knowing what comes next and what is expected of us. In my time away, I was reminded of the drastic turn my life took five months ago and how I could never predict or plan for what would be expected of me. I began to really understand this on day one of vacation.

> *Therefore do not worry about tomorrow for tomorrow will worry about itself. Each day has enough trouble of its own.*
> Matthew 6:34

This is not a suggestion or a cute sign for your kitchen. It's a command! So this week, I only saw what was right in front of me...and it felt good. The idea of "one day at a time" speaks to whom I serve. I have one set of expectations to think about and they are not mine. As much as it has taught me to let others walk alongside me on this journey, the only walking partner I need to focus on is ever-present.

As our beach vacation began, I had this sinking feeling in my stomach. Can I really do this without him? Can we make new memories at a place where so many other memories are etched in our hearts? My first night was hard. We arrived, unpacked and quickly headed down to the beach before sunset. The boys were in the ocean immediately, but I hung back to watch. I thought of what Scott and I would be saying if he was sitting with me watching our three goofballs. We would talk about how thankful we were that they were so close and, even though they were so different, how much they enjoyed each other. We would talk about each one of them, how much they had grown physically and where they were in their faith journey. Then there would be this sweet moment where Scott held my hand and we didn't talk...just whispered grateful prayers for our boys and our lives. It was hard to sit alone in this thought, yet good to feel close to him.

The week brought some old traditions, new adventures and new restaurants Scott had put on his list to try the next time we came. We visited old spots, played the beach miniature golf game that always turns into a competition with a prize, took lots of naps and got to see old friends/family (part of the Sellers and Colley crew). With each day, I felt more at ease... until Thursday. This was the 19th and the five month milestone. I woke heavy and feared I would be emotionally unstable all day. Every morning, I would sit on the back patio and view the ocean as I read my Bible and prayed. Thursday, I could barely see the words on the page through my tears. I think the 19th will be hard every month. Bob Goff's wife, Sweet Maria, says Bob is "emotionally incontinent." That is the best way to describe me - can't stop my emotions if I tried. Emotions are not sinful - they're given by God. However, they can tempt us to sin. What I know is not based on how I feel but what I know to be true. When I persist with this, my feelings fall in line with my faith. I will not push them away or tuck them deep down in my heart... that only gives them a hiding place so they can jump out at a different time. I will pull my emotions out and lay my guts on the table before God so we can deal with them together. When I do this, the enemy loses his foothold on me. He tries to use my emotions to take me to a place where my faith feels small.

This week I read -

> *In addition to all this, take up the shield of faith, with which you can extinguish all flaming arrows of the evil one.*
>
> Ephesians 6:16

I started thinking...the enemy doesn't just shoot arrows, he shoots FLAMING ARROWS! The definition of "flaming" is burning, blazing, fiery. Is it just me or does that sound like emotions? We could add to that definition the words "uncontrollable, unpredictable, overwhelming." The enemy uses the very thing God created for good in us as a weapon against us. On Thursday, I decided I was not just on the defense anymore, hiding behind my shield waiting to guard myself from what is flung at me. I am on the offense too. I will protect myself, but I am pushing forward against what scares me, attacks me or tries to sneak up on me. I want to live life charging the battlefield and not just holding the line. One of my favorite verses from a young age is *Romans 8:31. This verse asks, "...If God is for us, who can be against us?"* It has always made me feel strong and empowered. This week, when my thoughts reflected back to this verse, I wanted to run up and down the beach passionately yelling, "Thank you God for making me emotional and help me use this passion for your glory!!!" I promise the next time you see me I will not have on blue war paint or be yelling (this is a *Braveheart* reference), but know my heart is on the offense now.

In the pictures, you will see a table with Scott's beach hat. It stayed there all week with the exception of Cooper's occasional attempt to look like a dad at the beach. I would look at it in the midst of all going on and quietly whisper…"Are you seeing this?"

Thank you Marina and DeLaney for house and puppy sitting. I feel like Phoebe is going to be bored after a week with you two. Thank you Lee and Lucy for making this possible and being family.

Saturday, July 28, 2018

I woke this morning to thoughts of what this time last year looked like. February and March of 2017, we went forward with a plan God had given us. Scott was beginning the transition of stepping down as lead pastor of The Grove Church. It was eight plus years earlier he called us to plant the church, but now it was time to hand it off. So over six months' time, we did everything to help get the church ready for Scott to pass the baton. It was a beautiful transition, like two relay runners in sync, never missing a step. When July came, the last thing I had was taking a group of students to Bulgaria on a mission trip. Scott and I had prayed through this whole process..."What next?" Every direction God had pointed us in the past had never really come with huge prep time...just trust, so why would this time be any different? Scott had churches interested in him, but none in Knoxville. We felt strongly God had said, "Stay here," so Scott began looking in church networks and secular networks for a job. God knew we had two kids in college in the fall and bills to pay. On July 31st, he was offered a job with Knox County Schools as a high school history teacher. Lots of paperwork and orientation followed to get him ready, but he saw this as a new adventure. Scott never questioned..."Why not a church job?" He simply asked, "What will you teach me in this?" So this time last year, he was digging through items in the hallway that other teachers had discarded, learning how to navigate the red tape of the teaching process and developing content for his classes. Everything excited him, from meeting new people and learning how they functioned in their classroom to hearing their stories. Scott loved people and this was a whole new venue of potential.

Fall was hard because he was learning to teach in a

classroom setting. He was a natural with the teaching part and loved preparing just like writing a sermon…but the discipline and protocol was a different thing. Along with all this newness was going back to school to work on another master's degree in Education and searching for a church. Staying at The Grove would have been difficult for Josh Duncan, the new pastor. Josh needed time to establish himself in the church and community. We missed our community of believers and friends, but knew it was best for everyone. My sweet Scott never knew that this transition was part of a bigger plan to take care of us all. God's sovereignty will never cease to amaze me. I could tell so many stories of the people I have heard from that Scott touched in his six plus months at Karns High School and in grad school. This year, the 2017-2018 yearbook at Karns High School was dedicated to him, and I will receive an honorary degree from Tusculum University in December for Scott. That was my Scott! He made an impact wherever he was. He never cared about how much money he would make or what people thought about his career choices. He just looked up and asked God "What next?"

I will think often of my sweet man this week. Cooper moves out and into a house with five guys. I will be a little sad, but mostly excited for his new adventure. Nate will launch a new video project sponsored by Pilot (pilotprepsports.com) alongside his video internship with VFL (Vol for Life - University of Tennessee Athletics). Brodie will be prepping to start his junior year of high school and becoming the man of the house…the only man in the house. All of these new seasons for my kids remind me of Scott. He loved watching them venture out, take risks and do things to challenge themselves. I see him vividly in each one of them. He would tell them to never be afraid of what God calls you to do…the "what next" moments in life.

Never look to the left or right to see what others are doing... just look up.

I have also been challenged this week in my time with God to look up. Life can be like a hike up a hill. I can spend my time looking down at my weary feet (reminded of my pain, overly cautious with each step, afraid of stumbling)...or...lift my head to view the high road from God's perspective! This amazing view always takes my breath away. When I look up to see what God see's and desires of me, my focus is taken off the toughness of my path.

> *For I know the plans I have for you, declares the Lord,*
> *plans to prosper you and not to harm you, plans to give*
> *you hope and a future. Then you will call upon me and*
> *come pray to me, and I will listen to you. You will seek*
> *me and find me when you seek me with all your heart.*
> Jeremiah 29:11-13

So this week take a moment to ask God, "What next?" and remember to LOOK UP!

Saturday, August 4, 2018

Every Saturday I wake up, take Phoebe out, make a cup of coffee with caramel vanilla creamer, have some extended time with God and do my Saturday morning post. It has become not a "habit," but welcomed reflection on my week - a personal recap. It's funny that one of my lessons this week came this morning. I was taking Phoebe out and saw Brodie's car had been hit with sugar, BBQ sauce and something I didn't recognize (and didn't really want to know). My first thought was anger. I have been the participant and getaway car for many pranks over the years. Most of these involved shoe polish/car chalk, sticky notes, Oreos and toilet paper). However, this was mean and the ingredients could damage the paint. I woke Brodie so we could clean it off immediately and, even with my help, he was still a little late to work. The verses from my time with God the day before were hovering like a helicopter.

> *Reckless words pierce like a sword, but the tongue of the wise brings healing.*
>
> Proverbs 12:8

> *My dear brothers, take note of this: Everyone should be quick to listen, slow to speak and slow to anger.*
>
> James 1:19

> *Do not let any unwholesome talk come out of your mouths, but only what is helpful for building others up according to their needs, that it may benefit those who listen.*
>
> Ephesians 4:29

This was not done to Brodie by an enemy, but friends.

People in our lives sometimes do stupid things and the chances of that happening when you are a teenager is huge. But God calls us to respond in grace and forgiveness like he does with us. We got everything off before the sun hit it and it did any damage to the paint. When Brodie left for work, I went in to reheat my coffee and open my devotional book and Bible. Just like every day, God spoke again. In her book, Jesus Calling, Sarah Young writes, "Hold my hand and walk joyously with me through the day. Together we will savor the pleasures and endure the difficulties it brings." I laughed out loud! Difficulties of my day? Check! Now hit me with the pleasures.

By the way my little teenage friends...I know your moms. I won't rat you out, but I just may bribe you for help around my house. Just kidding...or am I? For future reference, don't post your shenanigans on social media. We parents are more stealth than you realize.

This morning was life lessons with high schoolers, but earlier in the week, I was having moments with Cooper. Wednesday was about us moving Cooper and his roommates into their house. There is just something about your first place. Independence from home, setting things up the way you want them, memories with friends - it is this amazing season of life that brings lessons, personal growth and so much fun! People kept asking me how I was doing with it. I am really ok! Maybe what helped prepare me is the fact that he is twenty minutes away, or that Nate lives in the house next door, or the month he spent in Arizona this summer, or the amazing roommates he will be doing life with this year, or...my God who has walked me through the roughest five plus months of my life. I am thinking it is a combination of all these things, but primarily the last one. God has prepared Cooper and myself for this new season of life. Just like those teenagers who terrorized Brodie's car last night, those six college guys living in the house with the red door will make mistakes. I was reminded numerous times this week that no matter what, I am loved by God and he will not leave me.

No one will be able to stand up against you all the days of your life. As I was with Moses, so I will be with you; I will never leave you, nor forsake you.

Joshua 1:5

God continues to change my perspective with big and small moments. I think He has always attempted this with me, but my holding tight to His presence allows me to see more clearly now.

Saturday, August 11, 2018

Every Saturday morning I wake with the thought of what one more week has brought. For twenty-four straight weeks I have shared my journey through my pain, sweet times with my boys, holy moments with God and life lessons. I have always tried to be honest and "share my guts" - not posting as I want you to see me, but as I truly am. Last week, I shared about a high school prank that involved Brodie. The entire day involved conversations about grace, forgiveness, thinking through your actions, apologies, etc. What I didn't expect was Brodie...well, let's say...not exactly giving full disclosure concerning his part. Being a parent walking through the brain farts of your teenager can be rough waters to navigate. These waters are not my first boat ride, but every child is different. I think God does that so we don't get cocky about our parenting skills. About the time we get one kid figured out, he gives us another one to "break the code." This keeps us humble. All that to say...in the light of Saturday's events, God brought out some difficult, hard to talk about but much needed conversations. It also brought up my feelings toward God: fears of disappointing, questions of mercy and grace, need for full disclosure and honesty to the core.

So many verses about God's love came flooding back. God not only loves me, but defends me like a parent does a child. He has confidence in me when I don't have it in myself and He isn't quiet about sharing that with me. When our kids make bad decisions, we have to remember to show them the way God loves us. Now, don't get me wrong...there are still consequences (just ask Brodie), but that is true for us too. God allows us to experience these consequences so we lose the desire to travel down that path again. But, what a gift. We don't always see consequences as a gift, but they are these life experiences we tuck away and pull out to use occasionally, sometimes even laugh at it. One thing I appreciate about how God handles our mistakes is the peace when it's all over. You walk through the stress, fear, honesty, responsibility and consequences, but in the end He says, "I still love you no matter what and I will never leave you."

You were taught with regard to your former way of life, to put off your old self, which is being corrupted by its deceitful desires, to be made new in the attitudes of your mind.
Ephesians 4:22-24

I pray that out of his glorious riches he may strengthen you with power through his Spirit in your inner being so that Christ may dwell in your hearts through faith. And I pray that you, being rooted and established in love, may have power, together with all the saints, to grasp how wide and long and high and deep is the love of Christ.
Ephesians 3:16-19

I will never be able to get my head around this kind of love that's never affected by circumstances and the peace that follows it, but I will continue to pursue it and learn from it. They call that the deep things of God. This week, the deepest part of me has tried to focus on the deeper things of God. Hard to do in the midst of a crazy week, but that is when I need it the most. Deep comes in simple moments like explaining to the guy at the Auto Zone why I have no idea what kind of windshield wipers I need and getting into a conversation about God's faithfulness. Then there was the lady at the government office whose simple question about my husband launched us into a conversation about God's provision and love. I have felt for so long that Scott's death defined me as "the widow," but the deeper things of God point me to see that sharing my story with people I meet every day in life gives purpose to even the smallest of moments. Deep things are not complicated or out of my reach, but they require a close connection to God, and that requires me to slow down, listen and see.

> *Deep calls to deep in the roar of your waterfalls; all the*
> *waves and breakers have swept over me.*
>
> Psalms 42:7

I have more to say, but reading my post should not take most of your morning. Who knows, maybe the "more" will show up in print. I do want to give you the lyrics to a song from the 80's that came flooding back this week. Christian Contemporary Artist, Wayne Watson, sang these words:

His gaze always passes
Through rose colored glasses
Every time he looks on my heart
And through loves forgiveness, through purity's fire....
I am my God's desire.

Please know, no matter what, you are God's desire. Feel loved this week and look for deep things in simple moments.

Saturday, August 18, 2018

I honestly start my post wondering how I recap the emotions, events, milestones and lessons of my week. On Monday, I turned 50! I feel like there must be a moment of silence to let that sink in... On Monday morning, I started my day with bittersweet feelings. I don't mind growing older...just thought I would be doing it with Scott. I thought about the twenty-eight birthdays I had with him. He was never extravagant, but always thoughtful because he knew that was my love language. It was a princess tiara and breakfast in bed, texts every hour on the hour that simply said, "Happy Birthday - Love ya," or my favorite from Starbucks (grande caramel latte with an extra pump of caramel) and a chocolate croissant. The key word is FAVORITE. He knew all my favorites. He was a walking encyclopedia of all the things that brought me joy. So before work, I went to Starbucks, got my favorites and went to talk to Scott. I promised him I would celebrate this amazing life I had been given and said thank you for walking with me for more than half of it so far. It was funny...thought about putting a flower on his grave then I remembered that he never gave me flowers on birthdays or any day that people expected. He only gave me flowers when I didn't see it coming. So, no flowers... just a Starbucks cup.

My boys continue to be a reflection of Scott. My favorites sprinkled Sunday and Monday...favorite movies, favorites ice cream, and tickets to a concert (favorite presents are experiences). The best gift was my favorite thing to do...just be with them.

My work peeps decorated my desk in black with LOTS OF CONFETTI (also a favorite thing to do to others). There were chocolate cupcakes, meals out to eat and "happies" for days. Wednesday night, I was given a surprise party with some of my favorite people and a cake (favorite color- green) and (favorite flavor - can you guess it...CHOCOLATE). My gifts were more of my favorites.

When I got to Thursday, I looked back at how well my friends and family know and love me. They know my favorites because we share our lives with each other. Tomorrow will be six months since Scott started a new journey. It will be bittersweet, but after this week, I feel like it will be more sweet than bitter. I could have spent the last six months closed off from everyone, but my people and my God refused to let that happen. You have all shared my journey through grief like you have all shared my life. That was one of Scott's favorite things to say..."These are the people we DO LIFE with." When you share your life with people, it calls you to be vulnerable, but the blessings are worth the risk.

I found myself realizing my struggle with wanting to be strong, yet humbly vulnerable. I want to push myself to do these overwhelming tasks in front of me to show others...I CAN DO THIS! However, I know that accepting help from my people not only shows my vulnerability, but my trust in God and total dependence on him for everything. I have come to the conclusion that the answer is somewhere in the middle. Walking *humbly strong* is the goal and the only way to walk this path is to *do life* with the Spirit of God.

> *In the same way the Spirit helps us in our weakness. We do not know what we ought to pray, but the spirit himself intercedes for us with groans that words cannot express.*
> Romans 8:26

> *I pray that out of his glorious riches he may strengthen you with power through his Spirit in your inner being, so Christ may dwell in your hearts through faith. And I*

pray that you, being rooted and established in love, may
have power, together with all the saints, to grasp how
wide and long and high and deep is the love of Christ,
and to know this love that surpasses knowledge - that you
may be filled to the measure of all the fullness of God.
                                          Ephesians 3:16-19

In my time alone with God this week, I was flooded with
more verses of his strength and love. I was reminded of his love
for me through so many of you. There are days that trying to
understand this love makes my head hurt. Simple solution...
God's love is made for my enjoyment not my understanding.

Once again, there is not enough time to share all the lessons
in my week. Just know how much I appreciate all the ways I was
celebrated. Thank you for loving me and letting me attempt
humbly strong as we ***do life*** together.

Saturday, August 25, 2018

When I look back on the last seven days, I visualize the streets of San Francisco with those ever-present curves. There were no moments to just coast straight ahead. Sunday was my six month milestone of Scott's death and the afternoon placed me in a hospital ICU waiting room visiting the family of a student who had been in a horrible accident the day before. In my moments before heading to the hospital, it hit me that I had not been in a hospital, much less ICU, since Scott. Brodie and I talked briefly about it and I have to admit I had this sinking feeling in my stomach. Of all days to do this, on my six month milestone? Then I realized that this was a baby step in my healing - to think about others circumstances above my own. For six months it has been about God, me and the boys. It has been my sole focus to just make it through each day. There were so many times I wanted to just be occupied by other things, but it seemed to always come back to our circumstances. This was not my nature, but the thought of adding anything to my life made me tired.

After I returned from the hospital, I sat down to thank God for allowing me to focus on others outside my family again. He gently whispered to me…"You're healing! Not forgetting... but healing." I needed this so badly. I looked at Scott's clothes in the closet and drawers. His coats hang waiting for cold weather, and I am sure I will wear them all at some point. Then, I opened the bathroom drawer. This is where he kept his toothbrush, deodorant, shaving cream, etc… Because Scott had staph, I had disposed of some stuff, but the other items just sat there. I told myself I was leaving them there just in case the boys needed them, but really I just couldn't clean it out. Well…this week I cleaned out the small drawer. I moved some of the items that were crowding my drawer into his drawer. The second drawer in the bathroom will always be "Dad's drawer." When one of the boys yells, "Where are the fingernail clippers?" the answer will be, "Look in Dad's drawer." This is healing...not forgetting...but healing.

I will always grieve my loss, but God's grace will sustain me. It's interesting that when someone is physically injured, we take note. We see the crutches, the limp, or the scar and we remember. When it is an emotional hurt, there is no visible evidence of the injury or the healing, so we forget. Don't get me wrong...I don't feel forgotten. My point is, my grief will always be a part of me. When I walk into a hospital, hear of a death or walk through a milestone...I will always be reminded. But one thing that I will also remember is God's grace. Paul talks in II Corinthians of the thorn in his flesh. There is speculation as to what Paul's thorn was, but we really don't know. He asked God to take it from him, but God's response was;

> *But he said to me, "My grace is sufficient for you, for my power is made perfect in weakness." Therefore I will boast all the more gladly about my weaknesses so that Christ's power may rest on me.*
>
> II Corinthians 12:9

Paul never said he would just suck it up or ignore his weakness. He said that he would boast about it so that Christ's power may rest on him. He knew that in acknowledging his weakness, he was open to receive all the help he needed and victory over it. God would use it!

> *Ask and it will be given to you; seek and you will find; knock and the door will be open to you.*
>
> Matthew 7:7

...you do not have because you do not ask God.

James 4:2

Sometimes there is more healing available, but I do not ask. Sometimes it is immediate and other times it is gradual...like a visit to the hospital or cleaning out a drawer. I decided that my continual desire to have joy again cannot be just based on my circumstances in the moment or long term. It must come from God's grace.

Each Saturday morning, I start my post thinking about my week and having an idea of what I will share. When I get to this point - the end - it is completely different. Once again... God knows what needs to be shared.

Love you friends! Thank you for carrying me through the last six months.

Saturday, September 1, 2018

It's September 1st and it feels a little like fall this early morning. The last week of August had me thinking about the next season. I am still moving pictures off of Scott's phone because I can only take the memories in small doses. I found pictures of past fall decorations on the outside of the house. He was always trying new things to get everyone into the autumn mood. One time he even checked Cooper out of school to help him get the enormous pumpkin he had purchased out of the car. Go Big or Go Home! He literally had his calendar marked for when we would decorate each year. I think Scott loved Fall so much because he grew up in North Carolina where the changing of the leaves in the mountains alerted you that the season had arrived. I grew up in Texas where we were still wearing shorts in December. A perk in moving to East Tennessee fourteen years ago was seeing all four seasons of the year.

Scott loved everything about the fall...the weather, the leaves and let's not forget SEC FOOTBALL! After his Saturday morning time with God, his Bible and a Krispy Kreme donut on the porch had ended, the TV would promptly come on and the kids would wake to the sound of college football commentators. You just knew in the Sparks' house not to touch the remote at this time unless you were turning up the volume.

We always tried to take a trip to North Carolina in the Fall. Scott and I would leave the kids with the grandparents and sneak away to go "loafin'." I learned this term the first time I went home with him. You might find it in Webster's but let me help with the definition. To us "loafin'" meant slowly driving through the mountains to take in the beauty...and occasionally stopping at an overlook to get a panoramic view. I loved this time with him because we slowed down and didn't talk about anything important or pressing - we were just in the moment.

Even though I loved visiting, I always seemed to struggle with the road. Now when we visit, there are three routes to choose from, but there used to be only one and it involved winding back and forth up a mountain for miles (something this Texas flatlands girl always struggled with). Scott would say, "Here we go," and that meant for me to lay my seat back, put the air on my face and close my eyes till we got to the top. I have gotten better with it over the years, but it can still make me queasy. We decided I would probably be ok if it were not for the road signs every few yards demonstrating how the road was about to curve. It's like they screamed at me, "HERE COMES ANOTHER!!!!!" But when I closed my eyes and leaned back, I barely felt the bend in the road. I trusted my experienced driver to get me to the top no matter what the road did.

You probably get where I am going with this, but my week has been like a curvy road sign. The thoughts of fall and an upcoming holiday haunted me. Thanksgiving was a favorite of Scott's. He would DVR cooking shows for weeks ahead of time to decide how he would prepare the turkey that year. I was simply the sous-chef who assisted in his masterpiece. I didn't mind because I loved watching him get so passionate about it. The thought of trying to do this without my head chef this year hurts my heart. I don't want to try. So I decided awhile back that the boys and I will do something different. We will get out of town, if only for a few days. As I started looking seriously at my options this week, I was pulled into this inner struggle that constantly reoccurs. Do I spend the money on a trip? What about the future? Don't I still have Cooper's and Brodie's college to pay for? What if a car breaks down? Is a trip a wise use of my resources? But experiences and memories are the best. Scott and I loved to travel and experience new things. Wouldn't he want us to LIVE?! And if anybody understands how we are not promised tomorrow...I DO! I felt this battle going on between my paranoid paralysis and passion for life. I sat in my living room floor and cried as I spoke these words to God..."I am responsible for everything and everyone!" God's response was emphatic - "No you're not...I AM!" I broke in that instant. It was like those moments going up the mountain, the signs screaming at me to watch the road because there will be curves. But when I hand over all my future roads, curves included, and simply lean back and close my eyes, I received a peace that comes only with total trust in my driver. God tells us there will be curves...pretty much promises it. He also promises to navigate us through it and to be a comforting presence. So after this week, GPS has a new meaning for me -*GOD/PENNY/in SYNC.*

> *Now listen you who say, "Today or tomorrow we will go to this or that city, spend a year there, carry on business and make money". Why you do not even know what will happen tomorrow. What is your life? You are a mist that appears for a little while and then vanishes. Instead you ought to say, "If it is the Lord's will we will live and do this or that".*
>
> James 4:13-15

> *Let us hold UNSWERVINGLY to the hope we profess, for he who promises is faithful.*
>
> Hebrews 10:23

Scott navigated that road flawlessly because he knew every bend. He knew when to accelerate to keep momentum and when to slow down to take the curve safely. One thing he never did was slam on the brakes because he knew that was the most dangerous thing to do. I am holding tight to that thought. I will not let paranoid paralysis take away my life. I will "hold unswervingly" to trust in my God who is faithful.

So if you have a chance to go "loafin'" in the mountains this fall, take a moment to lean back, blow the air in your face and close your eyes...unless you're driving.

I will share more later, but Thanksgiving is going to be amazing this year.

Saturday, September 8, 2018

I always spend Saturday looking back at my week, but Sunday seems to be a day of looking forward. I typically start the day by going to church, receiving encouragement and experiencing community with other believers. This has always been a time that prepares me for the week to come. However, Sunday afternoons can easily turn into my Martha time. In Luke 10, Mary is pointed out for making the decision to sit at the feet of Jesus while Martha hurries around managing details. I start thinking through my upcoming days...Cooper's Birthday, kids in my home for small group, short work week to get things done due to Labor Day and, to top it off, a colonoscopy at the end of the week! Yes - that wonderful preventative procedure that happens every five to ten years due to the fact that I am now **50**. My mind goes to the things that must get done early in the week, because I will be close to home on Thursday "prepping" (a nice way of saying - drinking nasty tasting stuff that makes you want to throw up, when in reality the results are evident at the other end of your body).

I feel torn between the Mary side of me that wants to just sit at God's feet, drinking in his presence, allowing restoration to my heart and emotions...and...the Martha side of me that wants to be responsible and get things done. Preparation is not evil (unless it is for a colonoscopy) - it allows for peace later on when potential for chaos hovers. The thing is... Jesus tells Martha, "Mary has chosen what is better and it will not be taken away from her."

I love the scene in a movie where one of the things on the character's bucket list is to be in two places at the same time. They always travel to a state line and straddle the border between two places. One foot in each state checks this off their list. This is me right now!!!!! One foot is in this spiritual realm where only God and I exist; the other foot is in the world he has called me - where what I do daily matters. My day is full of choices. I am called to do the tasks given to me with a strong work ethic that glorifies God...but what about that person who needs me to drop everything and listen? Even now, my puppy-person pulls me away from this post to go outside to just run around. She's not doing her business like she is supposed to but instead simply licking the freshly cut grass that turns her white coat green, requiring another towel job to re-enter the house.

What I am slowly learning in the moments where my Mary and Martha sides are duking it out is the word "BOTH." God is in my BOTH. He straddles the line in my heart and says, "We can do BOTH together. We can be productive and love people. We can do amazing things and have time together. Time does not work against us." Here is the kicker...

I have to learn to walk with my feet in both places.

I have to feel God's presence in my daily tasks and decisions.

I have to know that He gives me strength when my physical and emotional banks are empty.

I have to listen when He calls me to sit at his feet instead of moving on to the next task.

I do not write as one who has it figured out. I relax, then feel lazy because my list is long and I am overwhelmed with lost time. Next comes a task driven tornado that spins hard and fast then abruptly stops because there is no longer a source of power. It's not an "either/or," it's a "both/and." This is not a new concept, but one God has hit me with AGAIN! The amazing gift in this lesson was reassurance that God's presence continues to teach me how to be in two places at the same time.

I am the vine, you are the branches. If a man remains in me and I in him, he will bear much fruit; apart from me you can do nothing.

John 15:5

Be still and Know that I am God; ...

Psalms 46:10

So my prayer has become..."God, may I not only know you from sitting at your feet, but walking through this life. Thank you for showing me how to have my heart, mind, and body in two places at one time."

May you plant your feet firmly in things of heaven and earth this week...at the same time.

Saturday, September 15, 2018

This week God has called me to rest. My alone time with God, verses, conversations...they have all called me to rest. This fought my need to accomplish things. I don't know why I view movement as productivity. I am an "activity addict" and sitting still gives me ANXIETY!

Two and a half weeks ago, I took a graceful tumble down the two steps that lead from my kitchen into my garage. I had Phoebe in my arms, so just like any protective mother with her child, I held on to her instead of using my arms to help me brace myself for the fall. I landed directly on my knee, but saved my puppy from harm. I have stepped out the door and down the stairs into my garage thousands of times in the fourteen years I have lived in this house and never once stumbled...so why now? Walking out the door was not something I usually contemplate. I don't tell myself to make sure and lift my foot high enough to clear the lip of the doorway or to be more careful because I have on flip flops. I just do it because it's part of the direction I am moving. So, why do I have so much ANXIETY about moving forward when God has pointed the direction?

It is easy to hide behind my role as Mom and claim to be just thinking ahead... "It might rain so take a jacket." Planning ahead keeps me from being caught off guard. My anxiety tells me to plan for the future and be careful to scrutinize all my steps, investments, commitments and actions. I used to pride myself in being prepared for anything. I would compile this incredible first aid kit to take on student ministry trips and then be a little disappointed when all I got to use was a bandaid.

This week I asked God, "When did I become Debbie Downer? When did the exciting things in life become stressful for fear of what could happen? When did I start seeing all the pitfalls instead of the potential adventures?" I have subtly become a troubleshooter when there is no trouble.

Since Scott's death, I have seen potential for tragedy everywhere. I was so caught off guard. I don't want to feel that way again, but no amount of preparation can ever change what God has planned for us. God's answer to me has been rest! It is interesting that Webster's definition for rest is not just sleep. It says:

1. a refreshing quiet
2. refreshing ease or inactivity after exertion or labor
3. relief or freedom, especially from anything that wearies, troubles or disturbs

I really like number three…"freedom from anything that wearies, troubles or disturbs." God continues to teach me what it means to rest. This week it has meant stop planning for the worst and get excited about the potential. Don't let anxiety rob you of the joy God wants to give. It has been another lesson in trust.

I have been given a green light from God this week to move forward into the world of writing and all the potential tumble-out-the-garage-door, land-on-my-knee moments that scare me to death. So, pray for me as I learn to rest in God's direction.

> *Do not be anxious about anything, but in everything, by prayer and petition, with thanksgiving, present your request to God. And the peace of God, which transcends all understanding, will guard your hearts and minds in Christ Jesus.*
>
> Philippians 4:6-7

*Peace I leave with you; my peace I give you. I do not give
you as the world gives. Do not let your heart be troubled
and do not be afraid.*

John 14:27

Saturday, September 22, 2018

I have enjoyed my Saturday morning posts so much. They have been painful at times, but also a reminder of holy moments in my week. I think about how many social media friends I have. Some of you I see weekly, and some of you I have not seen in decades. Some live in foreign countries, but we are kindred spirits. Some of you I only know through mutual friends. Social media is funny that way. We follow someone simply because we have one thing in common...a mutual friend. I think it speaks to our need to connect with others. Maybe we have never met, but something you post might speak to me - so I take the risk and follow you. We desire to know others' thoughts and opinions. The hard part comes in wading through all of it to find truth. The funny thing is...there is no right or wrong in someone's story - only the telling of events. The events I have shared over the last seven months have been my story, my perspective, my feelings and my lessons. So no matter how you know me...read with no expectations other than hearing **ME!**

This week has been full of looking back and looking forward. Both brought new things to my heart. Wednesday was another milestone for me...seven months since Scott's death. I realized this week that when the 19th of every month hits, my mind goes back to February 19th. Each month has been different parts of **THAT** day. This month it was his hands. Scott had surgery on the 16th in an attempt to clear the staph out of his shoulder and knee, the two places it had settled and were causing pain. His hands were even more swollen than usual because of the amount of antibiotics they were pumping in him. He told the RN they would probably have to cut his wedding band off of him, but she saw it as a challenge and vigorously worked for ten minutes and walked away the victor. She cleaned it and handed it to me. I started to put it in my purse and Scott said, "No! Don't put it anywhere we might lose it. Just wear it until I can put it back on."

I am still wearing his ring. He had little stubby hands and I loved the way they fit perfectly in mine. I looked down at my left hand on Wednesday morning, seeing my band and his fit securely together on my finger and remembered those last hours in the ICU. I kissed him over and over again, but more than anything, I held his hand. I knew in a few hours I would not be able to touch him anymore, much less feel our fingers intertwined so perfectly. So all morning, I grieved the loss of his touch. - his tangible touch but, also the touch of his words and his heart.

September 19th moved on to things that life just brings, but as I looked at my hand all day long...I was thankful for the reminder to touch others. God took captive my thoughts and moved them from hurt to inspiration.

The mind of sinful man is death, but the mind controlled by the spirit is life and peace.

Romans 8:6

My looking forward came with the monster labeled "WORRY." I have stepped into some new and scary things. My need to plan everything and control everything gives me a false assurance. The thing is...planning does not give peace. I was reading about this false assurance in my devotion time and kinda treating it as another reminder, when God hit me with a "right now" life illustration. I reached to pick up my carefully placed coffee cup and knocked it over, spilling my coffee dosed with vanilla caramel creamer onto my new rug. The same coffee cup that, every morning, I am so careful to place strategically away from Phoebe's grasp or too close to my clumsy appendages. My coffee has this perfect place on the table beside the couch. This sweet nectar comforts as I read, journal and commune with God. As I jumped with lightning speed to quickly clean it up, I thought about all the time I took to pick out the rug and trying to remember if it was stain resistant. Then...I had to laugh out loud. All my planning to pick out a perfect rug or strategically place my cup didn't matter because...LIFE will bring the UNEXPECTED no matter how well I plan. God did not create me to figure it out ahead of time. He created me to ask him about everything as it comes my way. Trust is where my peace comes from.

> *The Lord will fight for you, you need only to be still.*
> Exodus 14:14

> *A man's steps are directed by the Lord. How then can anyone understand his own way?*
> Proverbs 20:24

Each week is full of teachable moments and I am learning to notice them. I sit in God's classroom every day and try to focus. At times, I am distracted by what is going on around me, but when I truly connect, his lessons open my eyes.

My Friends...you are not just "social media friends." You are my people. Take time to connect with God, those around you, and the lessons you can so easily miss if you're too busy planning.

Saturday, September 29 2018

Today, I feel a change of season. The cool early morning air whispered to me. Honestly, I already felt it coming, but dug my heels in a little. I just get settled into a place (you know what I mean - find my niche), then it's time to move again. This apprehension began last Saturday. Brodie and I headed to North Carolina to see Grandma and Grandpa Sparks. It was only a one day trip because of work and school, but we wanted to do it. As I was driving, I remembered that Scott was always with me on this route. He loved the mountains in the fall. It made me miss him so much because every memory associated with this journey involved him. The trip began with me putting the address in my GPS. Doesn't matter how many times I have gone somewhere, I used it to make sure I am not day-dreaming and take the wrong road...don't judge me, you know you have done it too. There is just something about having that smooth voice remind you to turn in 6.2 miles. There are three routes, and I thought I put in the one that kept me driving in a straight line and not winding through curvy roads. Guess what? I took the curvy road. Yes...me...who in the past had to close my eyes, lean my seat back and blow air in my face while Scott said, "Almost there." But I did it, and it was beautiful! I noticed things I never saw before (probably because of closed eyes).

I think God knew I needed to see I could push myself forward. The week ahead was full of "pushing forward" events. I had to go get my knee checked because it was still hurting and popping after my tumble down the garage steps. This kind of doctor visit always involves follow-up appointments, X-rays, MRI's and physical therapy (TIME and MONEY always seem to be the result). But I am going on a trip with the boys during

Thanksgiving, and I don't want their limping mom to slow them down - so I begrudgingly did it.

The visit began with x-rays, like I predicted, that caused some mild pain. Then came the introductory conversation with the ortho doctor I had never met. Visits like this always begin with history questions. How did you hurt yourself? Do you have old injuries? Where does it hurt? That is the pivotal question for me...because walking doesn't hurt, but twisting certain ways can cause me to break into tears. This is a perfect illustration of me right now!!! I can be fine, and then unexpectedly a memory or a thought can twist me just the right way and bring me to tears. As the doctor was putting my knee in all different positions, it hit me. I began to understand that healing doesn't mean avoiding the things that cause pain. It means taking them as they come and allowing my God, THE ULTIMATE PHYSICAL THERAPIST, to help me and teach me how to grow strong. The rest of the day I was in a lot of pain, but the days to follow, I began to get some mobility back. I still have work to do before keeping pace with the boys, but it was an amazing lesson about pushing myself.

> *No discipline seems pleasant at the time, but painful.*
> *Later on, however, it produces a harvest of righteousness*
> *and peace for those who have been trained by it.*
> Hebrews 12:11

Like my knee, I still feel far from healed, but I am beginning to see opportunities and not wanting to just give up before I start. I think God wants us to always be a little uncomfortable. I know that sounds weird, but it keeps us from being sedentary - keeps us growing. We have to remember to trust Him with the process and open our eyes to the beauty on the winding road.

It is always good in this pushing process to have friendships that give you a gentle kick in the pants. Thank you Sandra and Mary Beth for your feet.

As iron sharpens iron, so one man sharpens another.
Proverbs 27:17

As we begin the last quarter of the year and the change of season comes...may God use the painful moments to grow and strengthen you. May you also have friendships that give you that gentle kick when you need it.

As always...love you dearly.

Saturday, October 6, 2018

Today, I begin tired. The week has been physically draining, which is a change from emotional bankruptcy. In past weeks, I would look at my exhaustion and blame it on the journey my grief and emotions took me for the week. The last seven days were different. It was a mixture of just things that make up days in a life. Let me explain what I mean. My morning times with God have been sprinkled with reminders to rest, trust, be thankful, be vulnerable and to pick up the pace. The last one seems weird...I know. There are times God gives me a direction or path, and I commit wholeheartedly...at least I think I do. I spend time leaning over to tie my shoes or adjust myself in preparation while God is standing there patiently waiting for me to move...pick up the pace. He has already said, "This is our road to walk together so what are you waiting for?"

I shared last week that I went to see an ortho doctor about my knee. Taking steps forward in this process meant starting physical therapy and an MRI. This may seem small to some, but committing the time and money to this process was hard for me, not to mention physically painful. I have been walking through emotional pain for the last seven months and just now feel like I am treading water instead of drowning. So why put myself through it? God's simple answer was..."It will make you better."

There are days I want to just make it through the day. That's not asking much...right? But God has reminded me that "just making it through the day" is not living abundantly. I have to do things that hurt. I have to make hard decisions. I have to live. It's part of the journey.

In physical therapy this week, I listened carefully to all the words spoken to me. It started with "try this," then on to "how does that feel?" The final instruction that struck a chord with me was..."You have to listen to your body." Listening to my body can be confusing. Was that painful or just a little uncomfortable? Do I move on to the next thing or am I pushing myself before I am ready?

I can listen to all the voices around me trying to be helpful with their advice, but bottom line...it is my decision. Maybe I should say **OUR** decision. God and I have to walk these steps together. Like listening to my body, I have to listen to him. I have to silence all the opinions around me and listen to the only voice that matters. Because what makes sense to everyone else may not be God's way.

> *For my thoughts are not your thoughts, neither are my*
> *ways your ways, declares the Lord. As the heavens are*
> *higher than the earth, so are my ways higher than your*
> *ways and my thoughts than your thoughts.*
>
> Isaiah 55:8-9

So when my physical therapist had me doing things that did not make sense or pushed me to pick up my pace, I thought of my God. I pictured him chuckling at my apprehension, but not letting me off the hook. He was saying, "Your shoes are tied and you're ready to go....let's do this!"

Another lesson from therapy was not a new insight, but a much needed reminder. Pain is what the patient says it is! I have heard this a thousand times while working for hospice. My physical therapist can't tell me what my pain is...only I determine that. No one can tell me what things should or shouldn't feel like for me. But the beauty in this realization is - ***I am the one who feels the healing.*** I can tell when the pain begins to ease up. I can tell when I am getting stronger. I FEEL the victories. So my physical and emotional-self took turns speaking to me this week. My spiritual-self brought it all together when it reminded me that God's ways don't always make sense, but they make me better.

This week, I had physical therapy, not enough sleep, continued writing and editing future publications, chased a rebellious puppy, cooked a few meals and went to an amazing concert (Rocket Boys and Johnnyswim opening for Need To Breathe). These elements of my week were all physically and emotionally challenging, but pushed me to "pick up the pace."

I hope there is something in my shared thoughts that speaks to your heart. Shared journeys help make us better. Love you Sweet Friends!

Saturday, October 13, 2018

I don't really know where to begin this post. Can you describe your week as ADD? My thoughts, circumstances and lessons came at me from all directions. They all required time to process that I simply didn't have, so I may be chewing on some of them a little longer before I share.

Last Saturday, Phoebe escaped out the front door. Brodie was leaving for work and I was still talking to him with the door barely cracked open. Obviously, my mischievous puppy saw it as a challenge. She squeezed through the gap and hit the yard as hard as she could. Brodie, knowing how difficult she can be to catch when she is in full throttle mode, was worried because I was not functioning at full capacity with my knee injury. He offered to stay and help me capture the little white monster. I told him to go on to work...I got this. Most of the time, she just runs in circles around the house. I would just let her lap the house till she was tired. I smiled so Brodie wouldn't worry and watched him head to work, but honestly, I had a moment of panic. I tried treats to gently persuade her to choose me over her open freedom. It was a no - go. She would get a taste of them, but decide her time to be out of control was far more exciting. What came next for me was fear and worry. She began to stray from our yard to the empty lot next to the neighbor's house where grown up foliage and a huge drop into a ditch became a possibility. No matter how tenderly I called her name, she did not abandon her adventure. My voice became faint white noise compared to all the new excitement. At this point it had been thirty minutes. I was tired and honestly afraid she would fall into the ditch or leave the yard for the street. She is still very immature and believes cars are just big toys. Then it hit me - ask God for help. I was tearful and a little embarrassed to cry out to God for help catching my puppy. After my battle for humility, my neighbor's son came out with their dog and of course Phoebe went right to him. I asked him to snatch her when she got close enough. When he handed her to me, I wanted so badly to discipline her physically right there in the moment like a mother whose child has just run into a busy street. All my fear, anger and disappointment came bubbling to the surface. I took her inside, cleaned her up and abruptly put her in the crate so as to not play out all the scenarios bouncing around in my head. After I calmed down I got her out, held her straight out in front of me, stared into her eyes with laser focus and said, "I AM THE ALPHA!!!" I laugh about it now, but I seriously held my puppy with legs dangling and repeated that over and over. Then I hugged her, hoping she would understand that I love her and I know what is best for her.

Since our Saturday morning moment of clarity, I have seen glimmers of hope in the area of submissiveness, but she still has much to learn. I can laugh about it now, but in the middle of the storm, you truly see how your natural tendencies can overpower all rational thought.

Here are my lessons:

Like my prayer for help catching my puppy, I have to ask God for help with the small stuff. All of life's challenges do not fall into two categories...things I can do or things God handles. God desires to be present and to help with everything.

> *And my God will meet ALL your needs according to his glorious riches in Christ Jesus.*
>
> Philippians 4:19

Did you catch the word in all caps?

Phoebe's moments of freedom to lap the house were a safe place to run hard and celebrate. God loves us so much that he created us with a choice to love him and obey him. Forced love is not love.

> *Trust in the Lord and do good; dwell in the land and enjoy safe pasture. Delight yourself in the Lord and he will give you the desires of your heart.*
>
> Psalms 37:3-6

The key to that verse is, *"Delight yourself in the Lord."* When I do this, what I want and what God wants for me are the same. That has to be my starting point.

Just like my puppy, I can stray too far and be enticed by the unknown. My natural urges to do what I want to do can push me over the edge into dangerous territory with my emotions, decisions and perspective. This is when God loves me enough to grab me, look me in the eyes and say, "I am the Alpha!"

> *"I am the Alpha and Omega," says the Lord God. "Who is, and who was, and who is to come, the Almighty."*
>
> Revelation 1:8

This week brought some joy, some stress, and perspective about my needs. God has blessed me in so many ways, but my only absolute need is the one thing I already have and cannot lose...God's presence.

> *"Be still and know that I am God; I will Be exalted among the nations, I will be exalted in the earth."*
>
> Psalms 46:10

I always focus on the "be still" part of this verse, but this week it is about the *"know that I am God"* part. My week ahead is full of decisions and emotions that could easily push me to do things my way. In preparation I will wake each morning and remember....He is the Alpha.

Saturday, October 20, 2018

This morning, I looked back at my journal entries for the past week. How can someone experience so many things in one week? But, in all honesty, that is what most of our weeks are like - full of decisions, events, people and emotions...lots of emotions. My life is no different than anyone else's except for the perspective my grief gives me right now.

Yesterday was eight months. I don't have to say, "since Scott passed" or "since Scott started a new journey." There is no special phrase that makes that reality easier. Each month, I wonder what the 19th will be like. In all honesty, I have a little anxiety in the week building up to it. I knew this week would bring some new elements because of tasks ahead. Life must be lived!

Over the past week and a half, I took on some home improvement with my back porch and deck - nothing major, just pressure washing, paint and stain. These are all tasks I would have attempted in the past, but with my bad knee I had to hire some help. As the boys and I move the porch furniture back in place, I can't help but think of Scott. He loved the back porch! It was his favorite part of our house and not just because of his Bible, coffee and donut moments with God there. He watched the seasons change. He saw the places in the snow where the boys played or where teenagers sat around the fire pit. Our boys always protested when he talked about a fence around the back yard because it would mess up the hide and go seek games that involved the area between our house and the neighbors behind us. The back porch was also a place to eat as a family when weather permitted. It was relaxing and away from the TV and other distractions. When we were making plans to build it, over ten years ago, I wanted it smaller. Scott said he wanted it big enough to host a lot of people. He won that argument with ease because I knew how much he always wanted a "screened in back porch." Just as he wanted, it has hosted groups of all sizes over the years. As I look at it now with its touch ups, I think of how proud Scott would be of me for taking care of his special place. I have decided it's my special place now.

This week also brought an appointment with a lawyer to do estate planning. That sounds funny...like I have an estate. The simple version is: my will, my durable power of attorney, my living will, my life insurance, etc. - you get the picture. I went in thinking I led a simple life with not a lot of debt and not a lot of assets. After a two hour meeting, I went home feeling like I needed a nap. I was faced with making major changes to all of the decisions Scott and I had made previously in an effort to make sure our boys would be ok if we died. Once again, I was thrown into the world of decisions...alone. But as I left the fourteenth floor conference room of the lawyer's office with a thousand thoughts spinning in my head...I stopped! I took a huge breath and pushed open the door of the aesthetically pleasing building that led to the streets of downtown Knoxville. When the fresh cool breeze hit me in the face, reminding me that Fall was here, I remembered the verses I read on Wednesday morning.

> *Then Jesus said to his disciples; "Therefore I tell you, do not worry about your life, what you will eat, or about your body, what you will wear. Life is more than food, and the body more than clothes. Consider the ravens: They do not sow or reap, they have no store room or barn; yet God feeds them. And how much more valuable you are than birds! Who of you by worrying can add a*

*single hour to his life? Since you cannot do this very little
thing, why do you worry about the rest."*

Luke 12:22-26

As I walked downtown making my way to the parking garage, I felt God saying, "Trust me! This is no different than anything else we have walked through over the last eight months...we got this!" And that is when the PEACE hit - that consistent overwhelming peace that comes with God's presence. This whole "planning for the future" stuff has no power over me. My future is set and the same is true for my boys. So here is my formula... His Presence = My Confidence!

*Now to him who is able to do IMMEASURABLY
MORE than all we ask or imagine, according to his
power that is at work in us, to him be glory in the church
and in Christ Jesus throughout all generations, forever
and ever amen.*

Ephesians 3:20-21

When Friday morning "the 19th" came, I took my new formula to heart. God's Presence = My Confidence!

4:45 a.m. - I cried because I missed Scott, but thanked God that He gave me the capacity to love so much.

5:00 a.m. - I finished walking through my morning routine, very grateful it was casual Friday because I got to wear my new favorite kicks (red converse)...I knew they would help today.

6:30 a.m. to 4:30 p.m. - I left for a 7:00 a.m. meeting that would end with me darting out the door to meet Brodie at the dermatologist to get the warts lasered off his feet. Then came the dash back to work with Phoebe in tow along with my pot of chili I made to contribute to "Food Fridays" at work. I stopped a few times during the day to do some physical therapy exercises for my knee and received some sweet, thoughtful and, at times humorous texts from the ladies in my small group. During my drive home, I realized how strategic God had been with my day. The events, the people, and the laughter had allowed me to **LIVE** on October 19th. I thanked God for my simple but amazing life.

Saturday, October 27, 2018

As I open my social media app on Saturday morning, I am never sure what I will share. There are so many teachable moments in my week. I write everything down, because I am unsure what God wants shared and what he wants saved for later. Sometimes I wonder if the lessons are meant to be kept just between God and myself.

This morning, my app sent me a message. Most of the time these messages are reminders of things posted in the past, but today it asked me to update my profile. I never pay attention to that because nothing in my status ever changes (job status - unchanged, education- unchanged, birthday - unchanged, mother of three boys - unchanged). Then it hit me…*"Married to Scott Sparks!"* Even though it asked me to update it…**I COULD NOT.** I don't want to! I still feel married to Scott Sparks. Nothing about my life allows me to change that status. He is in the pictures on the wall, the conversations in my day, and the mannerisms of my boys and the wedding band on my left hand. His presence remains everywhere. Months ago, these moments were hard because they reminded me of my loss, but now these subtle memories help me feel his presence all day long. They are gifts of joy.

Honestly…it has given me a clearer understanding of God's presence. So many of my moments alone with God have pushed me to be aware of his presence. They have encouraged me to recognize, acknowledge, respond and rejoice in his presence. I want to be so aware of God all the time that it's as easy as taking a breath.

Thinking about Scott comes as easily to me as walking and talking. It takes no effort for me to place him in the middle of what I am doing or thinking. It comes as easily as breathing.

Do you see where I am going with this? This is what God wants from me:

To recognize someone's impact on your life so effortlessly.

To know what he would say.

To know what brings him joy.

To feel him close when you are alone.

To feel him **ALWAYS!**

God gently whispered, "Allow yourself to acknowledge my presence in your moments as seamlessly as you acknowledge Scott's presence." God's love for me was there before I knew Scott...it was there before anything.

Now I get why all my devotions have pointed me to God's presence. All the lessons I have learned about decisions, joy, thankfulness, worry and fear have been wrapped up in a beautiful present...**HIS PRESENCE.** This present requires some effort on my part to understand, but the instruction manual (the Bible) comes with it. With each verse, I understand how my present works and what potential lies within this gift.

The Lord replies, "My Presence will go with you, and
I will give you rest".

Exodus 33:14

Finally brothers, whatever is true, whatever is noble,
whatever is right, whatever is pure, whatever is lovely,
whatever is admirable - if anything is excellent or
praiseworthy- think about such things. Whatever you

have learned or received or heard from me, or seen in me- put it into practice. And the God of peace will be with you.

Philippians 4:8-9

You have made known to me the path of life; you will fill me with joy in your presence.

Acts 3:28

The virgin will be with child and will give birth to a son, and they will call him Emmanuel - which means, "God with us."

Matthew 1:23

I will instruct you and teach you in the way you should go; I will counsel you and watch over you.

Psalms 32:8

This morning, I was up earlier than usual for a Saturday because Brodie was taking the ACT. I needed to be sure he ate well and had everything he needed before walking out the door. Before he left, I prayed for him - no prayers for supernatural cognitive recall, just a simple request for God to bless his efforts. I asked God to help him remember what he knows.

I know God's presence is there whether I acknowledge him or not, but what a gift to be able to recall that as effortlessly as breathing.

God - Help me remember what I know!

Saturday, November 3, 2018

Each week, I start by talking about how much has happened in the week. I know that this is not unique to my story, but now I take time to look back so I feel more aware. I have always led a busy life, and I liked it that way. We are all drawn to activity because it makes us feel a part of something. Those of us who had kids playing sports year round don't know what to do with ourselves when there's not a practice or a game. We complain about it when it gets too busy, but we feel empty when it's gone. It is a good thing our God understands our back-and-forth emotions and patiently waits for us to make our way to the middle where we gain perspective.

This week was full of change and one very rough day. When Halloween falls in the middle of the week, it seems like we have this build up and then overnight everything changes. It starts with an excitement about parties, cute kids, funny videos and everyone pushing themselves to find the most unique and current costumes. And just like that, overnight - it's November. The carved pumpkins are thrown away, we freely wear flannel and the countdown to Christmas begins. It's not just the stores that overlook Thanksgiving - we do too. It's like Thanksgiving is mashed into Christmas, creating this two-month-long celebration season. Some even put up Christmas decorations on November 1st (don't deny it...you know who you are).

As abruptly as the change from Halloween to ThanksChristmas, was my abrupt change. I turned Scott's phone off. I have been saying I needed to do it for weeks, but had not retrieved all the information off of it. It sat on the desk haunting me every time I looked at it. Every time the charge went all the way down, I would plug it in again. It has been almost nine months, and I have every contact, note, and picture off of it. God finally said, "It's time Penny. You're torturing yourself!" So on Tuesday, I told the boys I was going to do it that afternoon. I told them if they wanted to call his phone or listen to his voicemail one more time, I would wait till they gave me permission. As I watched their numbers scroll across the top of the phone, each saying another goodbye, I hurt so badly that I could not breathe. Then slowly I received texts from them saying it was ok. Cooper sent a text that said, "Not yet"...then after another call gave me the "ok." I felt the same..."not yet" in my heart.

Even though I have recordings of his voice and laugh, I will never be able to call 865-466-8500 again. It was the last thing to delete. I have gone through months of having to take his name off things, but this was the last on the list. I cried hard all day long. I was grateful my office had a door because it was not pretty. When I spoke with AT&T, I heard that same response I had heard a thousand times a few months back..."I am so sorry for your loss Mrs. Sparks. We have taken care of it for you. Have a good day." I hung up and called his number. As quickly as October 31st changed to November 1st...it was gone. The only thing left was a message that said, "This number is no longer a working number." The painful stab in my gut and the raw skin around my cheeks and eyes from months ago reappeared. How can that feeling come flooding back so quickly?

My boys and sweet friends came to my rescue reminding me that turning off that phone was just a task. The sweet memories on Scott's phone and associated with his phone are still with me. All of these emotions in the middle of the week made me feel weak - and I hate feeling weak! God gently reminded me that it took strength to turn the phone off and that I am not weak. When I come to my God broken, it is an opportunity to communicate with the God of the universe. It is a privilege to know him this way. My neediness does not repel God or disappoint him. He flows freely through a yielded heart. My hurting heart trusted and gave thanks this week. It took the sting away to humbly ask God what I can learn from these moments.

> *Therefore, since we have a great high priest who has gone through the heavens, Jesus the son of God, Let us hold firmly to the faith we profess. For we do not have a high priest who is unable to sympathize with our weaknesses, but we have one who has been tempted in every way, just as we are - yet was without sin. Let us then approach the throne of grace with confidence, so that we may receive mercy and find grace to help us in our time of need.*
> Hebrews 4:14-16

These words encourage me. Jesus has "been there, done that." The point of this passage is not that he was sinless, but that he understands.

I had breakfast the next morning with Cooper and he showed me a video he and Nate had found on his phone from the solar eclipse in 2017. Cooper and Scott had convinced Brodie the eclipse had not yet happened...even though the time had passed. Brodie was standing in the front yard trying to understand why it looked brighter. They were laughing at him from inside and you could hear Scott's big laugh in the background. I needed that video so badly. It reminded me, once again, how much he loved life and loved to laugh.

As you walk quickly from season to season, from hard moments to joyful ones, may you remember it is not weak to yield your heart to a God who understands because He has "been there, done that."

Saturday, November 10, 2018

A few days ago, a sweet friend counseled me concerning my grief and her word picture has stayed with me as I looked back on my week. The last eleven days have been difficult. Milestones and memories have made me feel like I have taken steps backward in my healing, and that feeling has held a variety of emotions. Her words to me were simply, "Penny it is not about steps forward and backward...grief is like a dance." There it was...my perfect picture. Some moments are steps forward that feel strong and inspired, and some are a side-step with a pause to remember. Then, here comes the "step backwards"...which may be a painful thought or feeling. The key is you don't stay in one place, but continue to move in all directions taking each step as the music of life flows. The comforting part of my grief is that I have the best partner for this dance, and **He** desires the lead.

Brodie turned seventeen on Monday, and I saw a circle of firsts close. The boys and I have walked through all of our birthdays without Scott. We have been four instead of five eating Rita's chocolate cake, wearing the traditional "Sparks Birthday Hat" and choosing the events of the day for everyone else to submit to because...you're the prince or princess.

We celebrated Brodie's birthday on Tuesday because he wanted to have a few friends over on Monday night (Tuesday was Election Day and schools were closed). The head count went from a few friends to around twenty-eight teenagers. We don't live in a large house, but Brodie maximized the potential: ping pong in the garage, spike ball in the driveway, corn hole on the side of the house, and a fire pit out back with s'mores. They were everywhere! I will have to make apology cookies for my neighbors this weekend. When Brodie hosts, I try not to be a helicopter mom (hovering over). I stay in the background and simply observe. I noticed how he made sure everyone knew each other and felt comfortable. He had even recruited the help of Nate and Cooper to make a cornhole bracket on poster board to ensure everyone was involved.

Brodie is so much like Scott. He always desires to host people in our home, and makes sure everyone is comfortable and enjoying themselves. One of Scott's spiritual gifts was hospitality. You not only saw it in our home, but also at church and in the community. He always wanted people to feel welcomed, comfortable and important. He valued people, but not just in a surface way. He wanted to know what they liked to eat, where they liked to go and how they spent their time. He knew hosting someone meant knowing them.

The cold weather has brought memories of how he hosted me in our own home. I loved the way he would strategically start my car five minutes before I would have to leave for work to take the chill off. I treasured the way he placed all the essentials for my morning coffee next to the Keurig (cup, sugar, creamer, spoon) every morning. I miss how he would turn on the electric blanket right before bed so it would be warm when I crawled in. This is actually a really nice electric blanket that he bought me for our anniversary a few years ago. It has controls on both sides of the bed, so I could fire my side up to a toasty level four, while he kept his at a minimal setting of one, just taking the chill off the sheets. It was one of the best anniversary presents ever because once again he was thinking of me. He knew me and wanted to not only make me comfortable, but bring me happiness in even the smallest acts of kindness. So when Brodie called me this week while he was out with friends to see if I wanted a milkshake, I was once again reminded that he is his father's son.

My dance this week has brought precious memories of My Scott, but also painful thoughts of life without his small, yet significant, acts of kindness. God has comforted me with the realization that I will continue to see these moments in my boys. Like a good dance partner, God continues to navigate me through the moves this life requires. But in all honesty, the dance has made me very tired this week. My sweet friend who gave me the mental picture of my grief dance also told me to rest when I am tired - so that is what I am doing.

This week, I am extra thankful for my dance partner and so willing to let **Him** lead.

For in him we live and MOVE and have our being.
Acts 17:28a

Saturday, November 17, 2018

This week has been about looking back, looking forward and living in the moment. Holidays bring nostalgia for everyone. As painful as that can be for me right now, it also provides comfort with how FULLY KNOWN by God I am.

With Thanksgiving around the corner, my heart has flooded back to 1990. I graduated from Baylor University in the spring and began working at the Recreation Aerobics Center on the Southwestern Seminary campus. My roommates and I spent that summer transitioning our lives from Waco to Ft. Worth, where graduate school, seminary, work and grown-up lives would start in August. I had gone out on a few dates here and there, but never saw Scott coming.

I was working one day when this dark-headed North Carolina boy came strolling in looking for me because he knew I grew up in Mesquite, Texas and went to high school with Phillip Hearn. Scott and Phillip lived in the men's dorm on campus, and even though they had only known each other a few months, they became fast friends. It was November, and Phillip's birthday had some of the guys looking for embarrassing pics from his past. Scott heard that the girl Phillip dated for two and a half years in high school worked on campus. He came looking for pictures, but a few more strategic trips to the RAC on the days I worked and long "get to know you" conversations built a fondness for each other. There were no cell phones with social media so we could subtly stalk each other, just pure conversation. It was close to Thanksgiving and I had asked if he was going home to North Carolina. He explained that he was staying and helping out with a soup kitchen in Ft. Worth. I was going back home for the day, but returning on Friday, November 23rd. I told him no one should go without turkey for

Thanksgiving, so I was bringing food back with me and invited him for leftovers on that Friday.

We both remembered that Friday with fondness...and spoke of it every year at this time. He liked to say I asked him out on our first date...and I served him leftovers. I liked to say I felt sorry for him not getting to go home. He could tell you what I wore with a big grin (red mini skirt). I remember thinking he was nothing like anyone I had ever dated. I not only liked him, but liked who I was when I was with him. Who knew that one year, one month and five days later, we would be promising to love each other till death do us part. Who knew that twenty-eight years later, I would be reminiscing about that day *alone.* So next Friday, in the midst of shopping or time with family, think of those two seminary students (one in a red mini skirt) eating Thanksgiving leftovers with no idea what the next twenty-seven years had in store.

The boys and I are headed out of town for Thanksgiving this year thanks to some generous people in our lives. In all the preparations for the trip this week, I had moments of anxiety. I always did my planning with Scott. I thought about money, reservations, weather, etc.... Because it is just me and I feared forgetting something, I felt the joy of the trip being sucked out like a slow leak. I stopped and thought about an illustration I remembered from my time alone with God this week. It talked about how we can look at our days ahead and view them as paths complicated by splintering branches with too much to think about or decide. It then reminded me to remember who always walks this path with me no matter which way it goes. When I stop and think about my *Guide*, a peaceful fog settles over the path obscuring my view. I can only see a few steps in front of me. After all...if I trust my Guide thoroughly, isn't that all I need to see?

When that twenty-two year old girl and twenty-four year old guy had that historic meal together twenty-eight years ago, they had no idea what God's path had in store. They only saw what was right in front of them and they liked it! The trust involved in that peaceful fog calls us back to the moment.

I spent time this week thanking God that I am FULLY KNOWN by HIM - my past, my present and my right now moments.

> *Now we see but a poor reflection as in a mirror; then we shall see face to face. Now I know in part; then I shall know fully, even as I am FULLY KNOWN.*
> I Corinthians 13:12

I think it is interesting that this verse is at the end of I Corinthians 13...what is considered the "Love Chapter."

So this week with all the looking back and looking forward moments, remember to rest in the present with the confidence that in every moment...you are FULLY KNOWN.

Sunday, November 25, 2018

This is an early Sunday morning post. Yesterday's early morning shuttle ride to the airport, travel home and mountain of laundry kept me going with no time for focused thoughts. Our Thanksgiving trip to New York City will be remembered for years to come by all four of us for so many reasons. I want to say thank you to all of you who made this happen for the Sparks Crew. This entire trip was given to us by people who were generous with their resources and hearts. Scott and I had always agreed that experiences were the best gifts, but I always viewed it from the memories we made. Now...I see it on a deeper level - it's the things we learn about ourselves, those who share the experience with us and the world we are exploring.

I have to admit that planning the trip had some stressful moments. Being frugal yet wanting to enjoy, reserving tickets to sites, scheduling travel arrangements, making sure everyone had packed clothes for lots of time in the cold and wind, and stamina with my recovering knee injury...all kept me spinning. But when we arrived, God gave me this overwhelming peace about it all. Every morning, I would get up before the boys and just give it all to God. Then...I would quietly thank him ahead of time for all he would show me in the day.

Each day, I was thankful all day long. I paused in moments walking the streets of NYC, in the middle of photo ops and on the subway to just say "thank you." When we were starving and stopped to eat...I thanked God for the need to refuel because we had so much more to see and do. When my Fitbit would vibrate because I hit 10,000 steps and it was only 1pm...I thanked God for no knee pain. When I saw the way my boys would have a surreal pause while staring at a site...I thanked God because I knew they would remember this moment. When I saw them recall scenes from movies shot in the location where we stood and heard them say, "This is so cool"...I thanked God for the way it felt special. When I saw Nate take the navigational helm...I thanked God for his gift of leadership. When I watched Cooper jumping off things everywhere we went or dancing on the sidewalks of Broadway...I thanked God for the way he always makes everything fun. When I watched Brodie take his first subway ride and stare at everything with wide eyes, but by day two greet each moment with a "what's next" attitude while singing the words to New York by Sinatra...I thanked God for his honesty and authenticity.

I had this moment while standing on the top of the Rockefeller Center with Nate. We were looking at a 360-degree view of this massive city that was home to millions of people... and God felt so close. The fact that he knows me and desires to be close to me in every moment made me feel so BIG in the midst of such vastness. The only thing that held back the tears was the thought of them freezing to my face... it was 21 degrees. So at the "Top of the Rock," I was grateful for "My Rock."

I have read the verse where Paul says "pray without ceasing," but I felt myself practicing it this week. I found myself thanking God for so many small moments and in this constant communication, felt his presence. I was reminded that when I thank God no matter how I feel, he gives me joy no matter the circumstance. When my thoughts took me to Scott or our conversation and laughter reminded us of him...my heart swelled and I thanked God for the way he let us take him with us all week.

ALWAYS giving thanks to God the father for everything,
in the name of our Lord Jesus Christ.

Ephesians 5:20

Be joyful always; pray CONTINUALLY; give thanks
in all circumstances, for this is God's will for you in
Christ Jesus.

I Thessalonians 5:16-18

Come near to God and he will come near to you...

James 4:8 ·

I hope you take a moment this week to thank God for the gift of experiences. The things you learn about yourself and the people you are with are found in the small moments.

Saturday, December 1, 2018

The last seven days have been an explosion of memories and I don't use that word "explosion" lightly. These memories have come at me aggressively and unexpectedly. I knew Christmas would have rough moments, but I was also coming off a season where I had been thankful for so much. It doesn't matter how prepared or self-aware you are, when the explosion happens, you are still left with the adrenaline and the debris from the fall out.

After we arrived home from NYC last Saturday, I asked the boys to get the Christmas decorations out of the attic for me. It was a three person job and something Scott and the boys did every year. Later that night, Cooper and Nate returned to their houses with suitcases full of clean clothes I had just washed and a week full of experiences to share with their roommates. Brodie was also catching up with friends. We had been together since Monday night, and it was time to catch up with all their peeps. I was honestly enjoying the quiet. Love my boys, but sharing a hotel room with them for a week found me craving some solitude. These quiet moments brought on my emotional "explosion." The boxes sitting in the middle of my floor were full of almost twenty-seven years of memories. Could I do this? Could I open the boxes that Scott and I opened together every year? When we packed them up last year, I had no idea the next time they were opened I would be doing it alone. I opened the first box cautiously like I was waiting for a bomb to go off...and it did. It was the box with our stockings - the same stockings we bought before Nate was born, anticipating the family we would have some day. Then came the huge gold star tree topper that we let Nate pick out when he was two years old. At first, I wished I had waited to do this when one of the boys was with me, but then...I was glad I had these moments with God.

My need for God is what catapults me to knowing God intimately. I have to be honest...in the past, we would unpack the decorations and then work nonstop to get everything done quickly so we could put the boxes away and have everything ready to celebrate the season. This year is different. It is a week later and I am still decorating with things half-done. The days have been sprinkled with "aftershock" kind of moments and reflection has given some clarity. In the past, I seemed to take the change of each season like a gunshot to begin a race. Ready...Set...GOOO! My race started with a bang and I ran my hardest to the end of it. I was totally out of breath at the finish line, but as soon as my breathing returned to normal, I was ready to line up and go again.

This year, my seasons have been more like a relay race, similar to the explosions of energy when the baton is handed off for a new lap (season), then the pace settles. I find myself watching the runners around me, wishing I could keep up or even pass them. Then, here comes my coach's voice reminding me that I am not the same as the other runners. My pace, my stride, and my injuries make the race different for me. I am reminded to trust his coaching and how well he knows me. The final thought that fills my head as I round the last curve of each race is simply "same and different." A runner's muscle memory tells him to kick in that last burst of energy that has been reserved for the end of the race. However, each finish line brings the hope that there will be something different...maybe a new PR (personal record). The Sparks will have traditions and experiences that will continue this year. They will be same...but different.

Just like a good devotional transitions you each month into

a new theme, God has transitioned me in the last few days from thankfulness to love. I was reminded this morning when I began the date in my journal with a "12" that December will be full of God's love. This love brings me hope because it knew me before I took my first breath, and it will be there beyond my last breath.

As this Christmas season begins, we constantly remind ourselves to not get so caught up in the busyness that we miss the true meaning. My challenge for myself and anyone who wants to take it with me is this…

Remember to not only know about God, but experience him.

Take solitary, quiet moments to pursue him. My head knowledge of God can sometimes be shaken in rough moments if I don't experience his love for me.

To remember that he loved me before I was born and will love me eternally.

To remember that he doesn't just say he loves me…he shows me. Many verses encompassed my week, but here are a few:

> *Cast all your anxiety on him because he cares for you.*
> I Peter 5:7

> *May the God of hope fill you with all joy and peace as you trust in him, so that you may overflow with hope by the power of the Holy Spirit.*
> Romans 15:13

The Lord appeared to us in the past, saying: "I have loved you with an everlasting love; I have drawn you with loving kindness."

Jeremiah 31:3

Because of the Lords great love we are not consumed, his compassions never fail. They are new every morning; great is your faithfulness. I say to myself, "The Lord is my portion; therefore I will wait for him." The Lord is good to those who hope in him, to the one who seeks him; it is good to wait quietly for the salvation of the Lord.

Lamentations 3:22-26

Take time this week to "wait quietly" and take in his "before and after" kind of love.

Saturday, December 8, 2018

It's hard to believe another week has passed. I looked back at my journal entry for Monday morning and saw where I wrote, "This week will be full." I was right on target. It was not just full of activity, but lessons. My always and everyday lesson is practicing God's presence in everything - to be confident that his fingerprint is on everything.

A sweet moment in my week was decorating the Christmas tree with the boys. I took a deep breath as I unwrapped the first ornament Scott and I picked out together that said "Our First Christmas." As I watched them dance around singing along (every word) with White Christmas playing on the TV, I was thankful that first Christmas led to so many more.

I had many late nights this week, and it would have been so easy to be focused on my tiredness. I saw another journal entry that said, "I am tired but happy. God will give me what I need today...he always does." I feel myself moving into a confidence I haven't felt in a while. This is not a confidence in myself, but in my God who has not left me for a moment. When I feel my circumstances and my emotions taking over, I have to stop and remember being content is not about what is going on around me...it's about **WHO** I belong to.

> *I know what it is to be in need, and I know what it is to have plenty. I have learned the secret of being content in any and every situation, whether well fed or hungry, whether living in plenty or in want.*
>
> Philippians 4:12

And my God will meet all your needs according to his glorious riches in Christ Jesus.

Philippians 4:19

This week as I shopped for a family I had chosen to help at Christmas, I thought of Scott. The Grove Church started the Knoxville Free Food Market several years ago. KFFM is a place where, one Saturday a month, a family can come get a little help. While they stand in line, a volunteer will ask how we can pray for them. As they walk through the market, they are allowed to pick the items they want (as Scott always said, "truly shop") and are not just given a pre-made bag full of items and rushed out the door. Teenagers carry their bags to the car for them. And at Christmas time, a family can request help to provide Christmas for their family. All of it is done with the vision that we all need help sometimes, and God has called us to help each other. Scott felt strongly that no one should ever be made to feel "less than," no matter what their circumstances. As I shopped for my family, I thought about all my needs that had been met over the last months. I was overwhelmed with how much had been given to me and the different ways it showed up...so strategic in it's timing. I was pointed back to God's sovereignty.

"For my thoughts are not your thoughts, neither are my ways your ways", declares the Lord. As the heavens are higher than the earth, so are my ways higher than your ways and my thoughts than your thoughts.

Isaiah 55:8-9

God never meant for us to be self-sufficient. We all have needs, but the greatest need is for a savior. The richest man in the world lives in poverty when he lives without Jesus.

This week I hope you "see a need...then meet a need." You may be a part of God's sovereign plan in someone's life.

Sunday, December 16, 2018

O nce again, the events of my Saturday have pushed my Saturday morning post to Sunday. I wish I could be "Polly Positive" this week and tell you I am doing great, but I promised raw honesty when I began this weekly post almost ten months ago.

This time of year seems to have an underlying theme of remembering. The memories and traditions that accompany Christmas have been sweet, but come with a sting. I am not surprised by this pain...saw it coming a mile away. It is the predictable missing that comes with grief at this time of year. I see the words "Peace, Love, Joy" everywhere. I feel God's love for me in every breath, but like I said...if I am being honest... I have struggled with "Peace" and "Joy" these last few days. I predicted a busy week full of parties, events and a concert. There was baking, wrapping and planning, not to mention selecting the perfect Christmas attire for each event. I knew each moment would bring Scott back in small ways, but I had prayed for strength to keep moving. That's the thing about REMEMBERING...it doesn't always give you a heads up and never filters itself.

It was early Thursday morning and I was taking Phoebe out for her morning potty routine. It was dark at 5:30 a.m. and I had turned on every outside light to watch my puppy weave through the yard till she found the perfect spot. Something was different this morning, and as I got closer, I could see she was fighting herself. She was inserting both front paws in her mouth like she was trying to remove something. I could see the panic and fear in her eyes. I quickly picked her up afraid that she was choking. I did all my CPR moves starting with the Heimlich maneuver and finger sweep. Nothing I did helped her. I was terrified! I began to cry hard yelling, "God help her! I don't know what to do!" The memory I could not fight off was Scott's last breaths. Through my tears I told God I could not watch someone else I loved stop breathing and die. In that instance, God brought me back to the moment I was in and not what I was remembering. I put my hand in front of her mouth and could tell air was passing. She was breathing. I ran inside and placed her on the cabinet where I could see inside her mouth. There was a stick about the width of a pencil wedged across the roof of her mouth between her teeth. I quickly popped it out then held her and cried.

I wish remembering could be filtered. I wish I could only remember friends and family with me as I watched Scott take his last breath. I wish I could only remember singing, "It is well with my soul," in his ear and telling him we will be ok. I wish I could only remember watching my kids tell him all they had learned from him and promising to never forget. But...I remember EVERYTHING, and as quickly as my puppy moment, it ALL came flooding back - every detail! As I sat on my couch clutching Phoebe so tightly I was almost squeezing the air from her lungs, I prayed for God to take away the things I don't want to remember. He then gently reminded me that the pain is part of my healing. Remembering reminds me how far I have come and how my God has never left my side. My hope lies not in hard things being taken away or filtered out, but in the promise that I am NEVER alone - my God gives me immeasurable strength.

Yesterday was marked by an event I knew would be difficult, but good. Scott began working on a master's in Education at Tusculum University in the last six months of his life. This program was part of the requirements to fulfill his temporary teaching certification. In typical Scott fashion, he left his fingerprint wherever he went. Tusculum University called and asked if they could present us with an honorary degree (posthumous) for Scott during their December graduation. Yesterday, as I walked onto the stage with my boys to receive the degree, all I could think about was how quiet the crowd was when they introduced us, "Here to receive his degree today on his behalf is his widow and three sons." There it was again...that word... WIDOW! In the middle of fighting back the tears while hundreds of faces watched us shake hands, hug the President and pose for a picture...*I remembered.* Scott loved learning. He was an information junky and took every opportunity to encourage this in our boys. As quickly as that thought came into my head, I could hear my husband saying..."Penny... remember this moment. LEARN from it. Let God teach you what to do with what you remember." We returned to our seats, but snuck out a minute or two early. I had to stand in the hallway for just a minute to collect myself. I thought about all the eyes on me and how hard that was almost ten months ago. As my boys held tightly to me, *I remembered* again. I remembered standing at the foot of Scott's hospital bed observing them leaning over his body, praying and saying beautiful things in his ear. God showed me then that I would always remember Scott in my boys.

So today, I am grasping for "Peace" and "Joy" in my remembering. My hope is not wishful thinking, but rather a promise that heaven is on the other end of this amazing life.

To all of you who encouraged me this week in a huge variety of ways...thank you! I was reminded that, "I am seen with unblinking eyes." As you REMEMBER this holiday season, may you see the teachable moments in the pain and the joy.

Now faith is being sure of what we hope for and certain of what we do not see.

Hebrews 11:1

May the God of all hope fill you with all JOY and PEACE as you trust in him, so that you may overflow with HOPE by the power of the Holy Spirit.

Romans 15:13

Saturday, December 22, 2018

It's three days till Christmas and I am sure you are all getting ready for what comes next - Christmas services, family, food and presents. This season is all about looking forward in anticipation. Then after Christmas, we spend time looking back at the year before jumping into a new one. I have tried to be in the moment this week because looking back and forward have been difficult.

When I look back at all the good things that happened in 2018, the list is long: Nate graduating from UT, family beach trip, Thanksgiving in NYC, adding our sweet puppy Phoebe to the family...etc. However, it all seems to take a back seat to losing Scott. I will always remember 2018, as the hardest year of my life. With each milestone, I hold my breath and pray for God's help. I still have two more to go within this week - Christmas without Scott and our anniversary on the 28th. We would have been married twenty-seven years. I feel like I have run an emotional marathon in 2018, and losing Scott has been the mile marker for everything. My conversations with people and in my head have started with..."Before Scott's death…" or "After Scott's death…" My world has been drastically altered.

I have tried to focus on the true meaning of Christmas this season - reading verses, listening to music, watching shows that bring me back to God's gift in Jesus. My hope was that focusing on this would keep my heart from missing Scott. But today as I read about the wise men in the Christmas story, I gained a new perspective. When they traveled to see the baby prophesied to be the king of the Jews, they were in the moment. They had seen where it had been written in the past, but their focus was on the moment. They had no idea how much that event would drastically change everything in the future. As they looked on

Jesus' face, could they really see how big his birth was to us all? Maybe a glimpse, but that's it!

Please hear me say - I am not comparing Jesus' birth to Scott's death, but this event in my life changed everything for me. It altered all I thought the future would look like. The last ten months have been almost unreal at times. This morning, God whispered to me, "Trust me like the wise men following the star...look up." Everything God has done in me has prepared me to know what to do with this life changing event. When I have those moments where I don't know what to do or question my direction...I must look up! Isn't it interesting that scripture says the star the wise men saw went AHEAD of them?

> *"Where is the one who has been born king of the Jews? We saw his star in the east and have come to worship him."...After they had heard the king, they went on their way, and the star they had seen in the east went ahead of them until it stopped over the place where the child was. When they saw the star, they were overjoyed. On coming to the house, they saw the child with his mother Mary, and they bowed down and worshipped him. They opened their treasures and presented him with gifts of gold and of incense and of myrrh.*
>
> Matthew 2:2, 9-11

If I am honest, the thought of 2019, has me a little unsteady. But, like the wise men, I have a glimpse of things to come. I have climbed up on my camel and set out on a journey with trust in God's promises. I am full of unsure anticipation. Scripture also says that when the wise men saw the star stop over the place where the child was, they were overjoyed. I am praying for that feeling when I reach my future destinations.

Commit to the Lord whatever you do, and your plans will succeed.

Proverbs 16:3

We live by faith, not by sight.

II Corinthians 5:7

My prayer for each of you this Christmas is that you have an anticipation for the camel-riding, star-following moments God has planned for you. Saddle-up my friends. Love your guts!

Friday, December 28, 2018 (Bonus Post)

Today would have been twenty-seven years with the love of my life. I knew this day was coming and that it would be more difficult than the other milestones. All of the Sparks' family birthdays and holidays have been shared with the boys, involving memories sprinkled over many years. But this day belonged only to Penny and Scott. We never had extravagant anniversary celebrations because it was after Christmas, and we were always broke. Many times we would have to celebrate on a later date because we would be with family during the holidays. But no matter what, my sweet husband would steal me away for a moment, a kiss and a "happy anniversary." We don't have a ton of pictures with just us. Seems like when kids came around, it was about pictures of them or one of us with them. The very last picture is during a trip back to Ft. Worth a few years ago to visit our old stomping grounds. We are standing at the counter in the Recreation Aerobic Center on the seminary campus where we met. I never knew when that North Carolina boy walked in that day that God had big plans. So today, I wear the Duke sweatshirt we bought on the day he proposed. It was controversial because he was a Tarheel who was supposed to propose at the "Old Well" on the UNC campus. However, we had made a quick stop to see the Duke campus on the way - and when God whispered in Scott's ear… "Do it now! This is the moment!"…he didn't argue. So in the Duke chapel, on the sixth pew from the front, right side, Scott asked me to take this amazing journey with him. So very glad I said, "Yes!" Happy Anniversary, My Love.

Saturday, December 29, 2018

So I woke this morning wondering what God wanted me to share about my week. There is so much and yesterday's post on my anniversary was kinda an extra. When I opened social media, there was a reminder of my post from a year ago. There it was - the same wedding pic from yesterday, but what it said under it was the kicker. "Happy 26th to the one I get to walk alongside. Love you Scott Sparks. #myforeverduo" How could I have known last year that my "forever duo" would only be for 53 more days.

Christmas morning was sweet and painful in the moments before the boys woke up. I sat in my pj's with my coffee and only the light of the Christmas tree. I thought about Christmas mornings of the past. Scott and I would sit waiting for them to come downstairs together. Always together...whoever got up first would wake the other two because you had to come down together. We would talk about how much they had changed since last year, gifts we were excited for them to unwrap and how blessed we were. It's funny how that was the conversation every Christmas morning. We have many traditions in the Sparks' house and hoped one day our boys would pass some of them on to their own families. When they finally emerged at 11:30 a.m., we had a moment together. My heart was full.

The week brought a variety of thoughts. It's interesting how you think you know yourself and can predict how you will respond but...when the day comes, God has these nuggets of truth that cause you to take a deep breath and pause. Yesterday, on our wedding anniversary, I woke up and did my normal routine with a few exceptions because I had a house full of family. At one point, I just had to get out, so I left everyone to run an errand. I stopped at Scott's grave and talked to him forever. It was so good to just talk like we used to. I could predict his response to everything I said. I think that is what I miss the most...just talking to him. At one point, I could almost audibly hear him say..."You have to go back and join everyone. Let them help you through today." When I returned home, Cooper was there with gerbera daisies (my favorite). When he asked for red, knowing that was the color I loved, they only had pink. He said, "Well... she hates pink, but let's just go with it." I hugged him hard and laughed. I don't hate pink...just not a pink kinda girl. But who knows, after yesterday my new favorite flower may be pink gerbera daisies just because of my Sweet Cooper. The rest of the day was filled with food, family, football and games (wish I could think of a word for games that started with F).

Early this morning, I took Phoebe out and we walked to the corner of our yard where she likes to "do her business." There is this huge tree on the side of the house that backs up to my yard. Because Phoebe and I frequent this spot, for obvious reasons, I find myself staring at it. I watched the leaves turn colors in the fall. Then came the time they all began to fall with the exception of this one huge leaf. I know it sounds weird, but every time I go to take Phoebe out I check to see if it is still hanging. After all the rain we experienced over the past few days, I thought for sure it would have given up. Can you picture me standing in the rain with Phoebe staring at a tree? That was me yesterday. As I looked for it this morning (yes it was still there), I thought about myself. It's me! I am having to change with the seasons, but hold tightly to what anchors me. I could never have done that without all of you. God is my source of strength, but he has used all of you in my life to hold me secure and keep me from falling. As I read over all of your encouragement on social media and through text, I am reminded why I felt my husband say..."Let them help you through today." God created us to need each other. In the moments I wanted to fall, you guys held me secure. When social media sends us these posts from the past it always says, "Penny, we care about you and the memories you share here." No offense social media, but I am pretty sure that the things I share don't matter that much to you. But...to those people I connect with here...my friends, my family, my community... THEY DO! To all of you who have held me tight...I love you and thank God for you daily.

I will keep you posted on the leaf...I know you are all on the edge of your seats! LOL #leafwatch

As iron sharpens iron, so one man sharpens another.
Proverbs 27:17

A friend loves at all times, and a brother is born for adversity.
Proverbs 17:17

I am the vine; you are the branches. If a man remains in me and I in him, he will bear much fruit; apart from me you can do nothing.
John 15:5

I thank my God every time I remember you.
Philippians 1:3

Two are better than one, because they have a good return for their work: If one falls down, his friend can help him up. But pity the man who falls and has no one to help him up! Also, if two lie down together, they will keep warm. But how can one keep warm alone? Though one

may be overpowered, two can defend themselves. A cord
of three strands is not easily broken.

Ecclesiastes 4:9-12

Penny, we care about you and the memories you share here. We thought you'd like to look back on this post from 1 year ago.

🕐 **1 YEAR AGO**

Happy 26th to the one I get to walk alongside. Love you @scott_sparks #myforeverduo

Saturday, January 5, 2018

It's 2019, and this is what I wrote in my journal this morning - "I feel like a blank page." Sure there is the never ending list of home projects to be done, Brodie taking the ACT a few more times and writing projects; but I remember in the past, thinking about the future...at least two or more years down the road. It's what we do at this time of year - we look forward, make plans, start new projects and almost always change our diets. But I am not feeling it this year. Instead of looking down the road, I feel myself only looking two steps ahead. This "blank page" feeling is not me. Luke 2:38-42 is the story of Mary and Martha. I am such a Martha...I do not attempt to deny it. I am a planner! However, I find myself pulled toward Mary right now - sitting at Jesus' feet just blocking out all the other stuff. I feel my DNA changing...my planning/preparing nature has seen, up-close and personal, that it can all change in a heartbeat.

I still have those human moments where my old nature kicks in and worry comes flooding back. Yesterday, I went to take my car in to get the oil changed. I noticed two days ago the engine light came on so I thought I would just see what they said. When you pull out the owner's manual, you realize that light could mean 48 different things. So once again, I am at the mercy of "those who know." Of course it was MORE. I chose to only get part of the MORE fixed and consult "those I trust" about fixing the rest of the MORE. To paint a larger picture...this was at the end of a week where my computer and my printer were glitching...AND I had issues with Cooper's scholarship and tuition payment for spring. This entire week was a fight with my old nature. Worry about money running out and taking care of my kids kept creeping up on me. This is what brought me back...SCRIPTURE...GOD'S WORDS.

*For I know the plans I have for you declares the Lord,
"plans to prosper you and not to harm you; plans to give
you hope and a future.*

Jeremiah 29:11

Look to the Lord and his strength; seek his face always.

Psalms 105:4

*(Martha and Mary's story)...vs 42 - but only one thing
is needed. Mary has chosen what is better, and it will
not be taken away from her.*

Luke 10:38-42

*"I have told you these things so that in me you may have
peace. In this world you WILL have trouble. But take
heart! I have overcome the world."*

John 16:33

*Psalms 139 (entire chapter) but vs7 is huge...Where
can I go from your spirit? Where can I flee from your
presence?*

Psalms 139:7

*Psalms 34 (entire chapter)...The righteous cry out to the
Lord and he hears them; he delivers them from all their
trouble. The Lord is close to the broken-hearted and saves
those who are crushed in spirit.*

Psalms 34:17-18

Drum roll please...!

We live by faith, not by sight.

II Corinthians 5:7

Sight tells me to worry. Faith says God has been faithful and he will do it again. I think God wants to see me do what I can't do. He pulls me close in my humility. My BEST LIFE is lived as I deepen my dependence on God.

I posted screenshots of the lyrics to a song God has used in a powerful way this week:

Do It Again by Elevation Worship

Favorite lines:

You never failed me yet
Your promise STILL stands
Great is your faithfulness
I'm still in your hands
This is my confidence
Jesus you're STILL enough
I've seen you Move
I believe I'll see you do it again
You make a way where there was no way

So I am starting 2019, with a blank-page-Mary-squatting attitude. Praying for growth that is fueled by humble dependence.

Saturday, January 12, 2019

I began my post last Saturday by saying I feel like a blank page. This week pushed me to put some closure on things so I could begin to write that page.

We have this room in our house officially called the green room. The title is the result of the walls always being green - different shades at times, but always green (my favorite color). It began as a dining room, then converted into an extra sitting room. When we were planting The Grove Church, Scott had to work at home for a period of time so it became an office. When the church offices were rented, it briefly turned back into a dining room before the era of "the exercise room." The existing state of the green room is half office/half exercise room. It has never fully been decorated because the function of the room has changed so many times.

I have spent the last almost eleven months carefully thinking through any changes I make in my house because it's full of Scott's memory. I don't want that to change, but I also know that life is about moving forward and that can sometimes call for change. I have evaluated my reasoning behind even the smallest alteration. Last weekend, Brodie and I moved Scott's desk and rearranged the green room. The room is small for its contents and this new set up is probably not the most efficient use of space, but I just needed it to be different. Almost two years ago we placed the desk in front of the window so Scott could look out...but for me (self-diagnosed ADD), it was a distraction. Every time I sat there, I thought of the days after Scott's death where I made calls telling strangers my husband died and I needed to have things put in my name or emailed to my address. I sat there and addressed envelopes with a copy of Scott's death certificate in them to prove that I was now the responsible person. Everything having to do with that desk reminded me of all my "death tasks." Please hear me say...I LOVE THAT DESK! He bought it in Tuscaloosa. It was a kitchen table with a side drawer for silverware. He picked the wood, had it stained the perfect color and had a piece of glass cut to fit the top exactly. Scott loved having a large surface to spread things out on to work and study. I remember coming in and seeing him with four books open and numerous things out all over the desk. It reminds me of him in so many ways, but for the last year it has been a place to conquer a long list of difficult tasks.

For me to begin to "write on my blank page," I needed to have a space I claim as my own. The desk now sits in the corner of the room...a space I claimed. With this move came the task of sorting through the last two piles of stuff that sat next to the desk. When Scott died, I brought every file, box and container that stored important things into the green room. I had to find numerous documents, so I put everything in one place to make it easier to find what was needed. I had worked my way down to the last two piles in October, then just had to stop. I was tired. Even though my organized nature screamed at me every time I passed by the piles...I just didn't have it in me. With the move of the desk came the return of sifting through the piles. They haunted me because I knew there were memories all throughout the stack of files. I sat in the floor with the "last two piles", took a deep breath and began.

Scott kept everything! He disguised his hoarding by placing every item in a labeled file. I found the file with all the instruction manuals, including the Little Tikes jungle gym Nate was given when he was two years old, and the lawn mower we owned when we were first married. There were times I was thankful he kept everything, but he never went back to throw anything out we no longer owned...LOL. But then came the files of memories...our marriage license, the receipt for my engagement ring and wedding rings, handmade father's day and birthday cards the boys had made him, cards and notes I had given him (even just scratch pieces of paper where I had told him I was praying for him) etc... I found a file labeled "correspondence with students." It was full of letters written from students dating back to our seminary days. Some were written to both of us and some to us individually. They were full of thank-you's. Once again I was reminded of the legacy my husband left behind. The words I read were:

"Thank you for not giving up on me."

"Thank you leading me to Christ."

"Thank you for showing me how to be a godly husband and father."

"Thank you for pursuing me even when I ran."

For those of you reading this post now who wrote some of those letters and notes, please know how much he cherished your words.

Thank-you's can be powerful and I was reminded this weekend that I need to not only be grateful, but I need to say "Thank You" more often. When God brings a memory or someone to my heart, I need to tell them the impact their lives, words or moments shared had in my life. This inspired me to write a letter to someone saying thank you for a teachable moment over thirty years ago. It was not easy tracking down the address, but the effort was worth it.

When we are thankful for the people God uses in our lives,

we are reminded of his constant presence. He has purpose in our everyday "spare moments." Reading those letters brought me back to so many moments that I could have never known would mean so much. God's sovereignty shows up in his perfect timing. I took my thankfulness to a new level this week. I thanked God for the answers he has already set in motion. Constantly stating my concerns to God can make me tense if I do not go ahead and thank him for the answers and the promises I know are coming.

> *Be still and know that I am God; I will be exalted among the nations, I will be exalted in the earth.*
> Psalms 46:10

> *...If God is for us who can be against us?*
> Romans 8:31b

> *I thank my God every time I remember you. In all my prayers for all of you, I always pray with joy because of your partnership in the gospel from the first day until now.*
> Philippians 1:3

> *Devote yourselves to prayer, being watchful and thankful.*
> Colossians 4:2

My week was so full of thought. All I really know is that my heart is thankful for God ordained people and moments from my past...and that God knows exactly what will fill the blank pages of my future.

Saturday, January 19, 2019

This week several people have asked me how I'm doing and my answer has been..."My thoughts are thick." Weird answer, but in my perspective it has been the best way to describe the last 168 hours. When something is thick, it doesn't always mean heavy, just very full or dense - a lot crammed into a limited space. I have condensed so much thought into my "sun-up to sun-downs." Not sure that all my weeks can handle this thickness, but it was good to take full advantage of the gift in my unrepeatable days.

I knew the tasks in my week ahead of time and my personal goal was to be prepared. Doesn't sound bad except the part where I forget that my days belong to God. I can wake early and rehearse the events of the day and my part in them, but ultimately God has this plan that may not read the same as mine. I was reminded to stop rehearsing my day and simply live it *once*.

Monday, I scratched off the last thing on a tear stained list I composed almost eleven months ago. Today it has been eleven months...! Hard to say out loud, but I have been thinking about it all week. I have remembered myself broken and unsure, but still trying to write down all the things...my "death tasks"...that needed to be done because Scott was no longer the leader in our home...*I WAS!* I kept thinking about the responsibility he must have felt to shoulder all this. The last item to scratch off was signing all the papers that make decisions for my kids if something happens to me: my will, power of attorney, healthcare proxy, living will, etc… The thought of my boys having to walk through the list of things I have scratched off this year has given me pause. All the unexpected details that show up when someone dies can compete with your grief for attention.

I can honestly say that the peace that comes from trusting God to care for me has come easier than peace that passes all understanding. My "thick thoughts" want to understand. I am not doubting God, but I wish I understood sometimes.

I was reminded of an illustration this week. Looking out over a roaring sea, I witness waves coming at me. They seem big and beyond reason, having no pattern to their tossing. But as they get closer, their size shrinks, and what seemed overwhelming, becomes manageable. The tasks of the last eleven months felt like those huge distant waves making their way closer to me. As I look back over each month, I see this shrinking process wrapped up in my perspective...my God eyes. As each thing rolled at me with force, God gave me his perspective...his eyes...and they seemed so much smaller. With God's eyes came his peace and his comfort. All these elements have made understanding take a back seat. Believe me when I say my craving for understanding is still there, but God is patient with me.

> *And the peace of God which transcends all understanding*
> *will guard your hearts and minds in Christ Jesus.*
> Philippians 4:7

On top of my closure this week, there have been moments with a friend celebrating God's timing and moments with a different friend hurting from loss. My conversation and prayers have revolved around UNDERSTANDING! The front end of understanding seems to always be frustrating, but the back end seems to produce a thankful heart. The hard part is the living in the middle. For me the solution has been *Hebrews 12:2 - "fixing my eyes on the author and perfector of my faith."*

As I enter into the last month of my first year without Scott, I am apprehensive. I feel my "thick thoughts" waiting on me in every quiet moment. My prayers are the verses that have saturated me over the last eleven months. I will pursue my God vigorously over these thirty-one days knowing that He will give me His strength, His Love and His eyes.

> *My heart says to you, "Seek his face." Your face Lord,*
> *I will seek.*

Psalms 27:8

I have so many more thoughts, but chewing on these will take enough time. Thank you for being my friends.

Saturday, January 26, 2019

I would love to start my post with poetic words like..."as I take pen in hand to write you"...but it is a gentle tap on my phone screen that becomes the avenue I choose to share myself today. This is no made-for-TV movie moment where I sit at a desk with a pensive look on my face (WOW - I have watched way too many Hallmark movies). It's just me, sitting on the corner of the couch, with Phoebe curled up next to me in the same spot I have claimed for almost every one of my 49 (and a few extra) Saturday Morning posts.

As the one year anniversary of Scott's death approaches, I think about the journey. I could say I thought about my stages of grief, the lessons I have learned or even my life-altering perspective on what it means to be loved by God. All this is true but this morning my thoughts land on people. The other day I told someone that I felt like everyone has grieved with me this year.

This journey we call life was never meant to be walked alone. In all honesty, some weeks it has been difficult to show my guts while other weeks it was a relief to just talk or type about my unsure and very insecure moments. I have been asked a thousand times this year, by friends and strangers, "How do you do it?" My response is the same every time..."My God, My Faith and My Friends." It's funny that almost a year later, God pushes me to tell my story. Even this week, I was on the phone with a cable provider and God gave me an opportunity to share my story and share his glory with a stranger (just may have received a discount and a few extra channels).

I know this is the long way around to introducing my thoughts for the week, but honestly my fingers are still hesitant to type the words on my screen. I shared in subtle ways this year that I have been encouraged to write. I have given little tidbits here and there but still walked the border of commitment. I feel like a child kicking and screaming as she approaches something she is being forced to do that terrifies her. The one thing that helps me stand up to my fear is God's voice is saying... "Let me use your journey to help others." In that moment, I know that if only a handful of people buy my book but God uses my story for his glory, then it was worth it.

So...I will be publishing my first year of posts to begin this process. My first push back was simple. Why would people want to buy something they can get free on social media? But I don't think this is about just my social media friends. It is about the people I don't know who need to see an honest walk through life's roughest moments. My thoughts this year have not only been about my grief but my life. That is why the title will not have the word death or grief in it.

God brought me to this verse over and over this week.

> *"I have told you these things, so that in me you may have peace. In this world YOU WILL HAVE TROUBLE. But take heart! I have overcome the world."*
> John 16:33

Jesus is talking to his disciples to prepare them for what is coming. He flat out tells them...YOU WILL HAVE TROUBLE! I don't believe that I am through with trials or tough times in life. This year has been the ultimate trial experience in every way, but life is not a "one and done" when it comes to troubles. We are told over and over in scripture that this life is full of them. But the kicker is the last part of the verse: "But take heart! I have overcome the world."

What I hope I have communicated this year is this...no

matter what life brings or how you feel about it...God is bigger and he promises his presence through it all. I hope my posts have been more about life than death.

For to me, to live is Christ and to die is gain.

Philippians 1:21

Please continue to pray for me as I dip my toe into the publishing pond. I have committed not only to this project, but a second one to follow. Several people have asked what I will title my book. I have thought about...*My Saturday Morning Posts* - nothing dramatic, eloquent or catchy. Scott had an opinion about titles and t-shirt slogans - If you have to spend a lot of time explaining them, it's too much. Keep it simple. Sounds like good advice.

As always...thank you for putting on your walking shoes with me.

Saturday, February 2, 2019

O nce again, the shaded words that are supposed to prompt you to begin your post..."What's on your mind"...have profound meaning in my week. The transparent raw feelings that consumed the beginning of my week were wrapped up in this four letter word...FEAR. I have walked through so much this year, so why now? What am I afraid of? My answer was... FEBRUARY!!!!! I hate February! There - I said it! I have always told my boys not to throw the word "hate" around. It is a strong word that is usually accompanied by heavy baggage - suitcase full of rocks kind of baggage. But If I am being honest, like I promised I would be, it is how I feel. All week long, I felt it coming. The countdown to February 19th - the one year anniversary of Scott's death - would begin.

God has carried me, held my hand, walked beside me and at times given me a swift kick this year. Through every moment I never doubted I would make it...and I don't now. What I fear about the next few days is the pain that comes from remembering. I have been in unbearable physical pain and it doesn't hold a candle to the emotional pain I felt last year. Like a surgeon's knife to skin that has not been deadened, I felt every moment. What comes with February, is remembering the days leading up to the 19th: the week he was home sick, the trip to the doctor because he could no longer bear the pain, spending all night in the ER, and yes...Valentine's Day. I spent that day watching him in horrible pain and doing things for my husband I had never done in our twenty-six years of marriage. With each task that day he would smile and sarcastically say, "Happy Valentine's Day...this is one for the books." Yep...our last one. I am afraid of feeling that pain all over again. I know I keep using the surgery analogy...but it's like having painful surgery on a part of your body knowing that just when you begin to heal the same surgery waits for another part of you. There is no way to fool yourself into thinking it won't hurt as badly.

Bottom Line: February is gonna hurt! Scott and I use to talk about problems and solutions. In all those years of side-by-side we heard so many people express their problems. You know...the ones that the minister and his wife needed to fix. I loved it when Scott would just look at them and very graciously say, "Do you have any solutions?" **Love that Man!!!** This whole week I thought about that...what is my solution? I will not bottle my emotions only to let them escape later. I will not keep myself from feeling. I will not let my fear of pain rob my joy. So what do I do? The pain is going to be there. Fear of my pain will rush at me like a warrior on the battlefield. It's going to happen! A warrior's best weapon is their mind. So here is my battle strategy...

We demolish arguments and every pretension that sets itself up against the knowledge of God, and we take CAPTIVE every thought to make it obedient to Christ.
II Corinthians 10:5

With your help I can advance against the troop, with my God I can scale a wall.
Psalms 18:28

Do not conform any longer to the pattern of this world, but be transformed by the renewing of your mind...
Romans 12:2

I began this post telling you about that four letter word... FEAR. Going to end it with another four letter word...MIND. There is a battle that wages for my mind. Over and over scripture calls me to protect it, renew it and take captive my thoughts. This is for good reason...it's connected to my heart. When my mind is saturated with God's presence my heart joins in and what I know to be true comforts in a way that only my Divine Creator can. So in my February days, I will take captive the painful thoughts that creep up to attack in spare moments and hand them over to the Protector of my Heart. Thank you God for taking my small self and making me a warrior (having a David and Goliath moment)!

I still have strong feelings about February for now, but I will say this... the chocolate that comes with it is a good thing.

For all of you who have grieved with me this past year... thank you for courageously fighting alongside me. This month we will put on our war paint and wage war in the battle for our mind knowing the fight for our heart is worth it.

So much love for you...

Saturday, February 9, 2019

I was awake early this morning to make sure Brodie was up, well fed and had everything ready to take the ACT. He is my third child, so this ain't my first rodeo (sorry...had to say it...I'm from Texas). The anxiety that comes with testing brings so many lessons. As he drove away I thought about what we prayed for before he left. We asked God to calm his heart and give him peace. We asked God to help him remember what he knows...no huge miracle...just bless his efforts. I watched his car leave our street and thought about my last prayer for him..."use this moment as a lesson for things to come." That's when God hit me with it..."That goes for you too, Penny."

Every day of February begins with me asking for just enough to walk me though the day. I am letting go of the need to prepare myself for the days ahead and just focusing on THE DAY ahead. Since Scott passed, I have dealt with phone calls from people who don't know - usually medical appointments, random things Scott had registered for or surveys. Each time has a sting to it. Honestly, I sometimes don't respond because I don't want to explain again. This week I received one that had to be called back.

Almost twenty years ago, when we were living in Tuscaloosa, there was a bone marrow registry drive. Well, twelve years ago this month Scott and I drove to Vanderbilt so he could donate bone marrow to someone he was matched with through this registry. I remembered the months of testing they did to make sure he was a perfect match with this man in his sixties, dying of cancer. All we knew about him was that he was a grandfather. I remember the pain Scott was in after they drilled holes into his lower back to remove a liter of bone marrow. I remember the weeks and months before he was completely himself again.

When people asked Scott why he went through all this for someone he had never met, his answer was simple: "If you knew you could do something that could save someone's life, wouldn't you do it too?" There you have it!

As I called the National Bone Marrow Registry back to tell them Scott would not be able to participate in the ongoing research, I couldn't help but pause. He sacrificed to give this man more years with his grandkids - to be able to have experiences that Scott would never have himself. When we truly lay ourselves down as offerings for others and say, "It is about you, not me," we don't see what we are giving up...we see what others are gaining. Reminds me of the cross...

Another lesson from my week came barreling in with strategic timing. I had some low moments where my wandering mind strayed. In the midst of one of these ponders, I opened an email. I was fearful just seeing the title because I knew it was going to come with a request for a large sum of money. I was already riding the struggle bus that day, but I held my breath and clicked on the message. As I scrolled to the bottom I realized that this request ended with a big fat $0 balance. Someone who hardly knew me chose to provide a service that could have produced a LARGE amount...but they wrote "no charge" at the bottom of the statement. Once again Scott's words rang true: "If you know you could help someone, wouldn't you?" I sat and cried over the generosity! God continues to remind me of his sovereignty and care for me. I feel like Peter in Matthew 14... walking on water out to Jesus. He is doing fine until he gets distracted by the wind and begins to sink. Jesus then catches him and they get back in the boat together. My circumstances can distract me and pull my eyes off my God. The part I love is how Jesus catches Peter before he sinks and restores him to safety. Over and over God shows up even when I lose focus. His faithfulness is not dependent on mine.

My lessons this week are the prayers I prayed for Brodie this morning...I just realized they are prayers for myself.

God calm my heart and give me peace.

God help me remember what I know.

God bless my efforts.

God use my moments as lessons for things to come.

Take a minute to read Matthew 14:22-33. I would type it in this post but I think the effort to look it up will be worth it. God calls us ALL to WALK ON WATER but also promises to catch us when we lose focus.

Thank you for your continued prayers. I feel them as I take on each day of this month. As always...unimaginable love for you all.

Thursday, February 14, 2019

Scott's Legacy of thoughtfulness lives on in My Boys. You taught them well, My Love. #favoriteflowers #favoritepeople

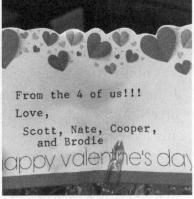

From the 4 of us!!!
Love,
Scott, Nate, Cooper, and Brodie

happy valentine's day

Saturday, February 16, 2019

This morning, my thoughts allowed for a little extra sleep so I took advantage. I entered into this week with an anxious heart. The unknown can scare you but it can also be full of intrigue. I have shared my fear of reliving moments from this time last year and my need to take captive my thoughts. So many of you have called, sent texts and messages, prayed over me and encouraged my heart. With the theme of this Valentines Week being love...I need to say...I have felt so loved. I was reminded that God manifests his love for me through others. Yet, I didn't hear those three words, "I Love You," any more than usual this week. They are spoken to me with overwhelming frequency.

Every Monday night, I eat dinner with my Sparks Men. We may only catch each other for a few hours, but it's always good. I may cook, we may go out to eat, but no matter what...it's our time. I have always tried to be intentional to have spots of time with my boys individually. Last Monday, I caught Cooper for a moment to ask how he felt about the upcoming anniversary of Scott's death. I needed to hear his words..."I want to celebrate Dad." My struggle was not his. On Wednesday, I sat in my small group Bible study and heard the same words come out of Leah Burton's mouth: "Penny, my prayer for you is that the 19th will not be about remembering your loss on that day, but celebrating Scott and his impact on this earth." Once again... these are words I needed to hear.

As so many of you saw, my celebrating Scott began on Thursday (Valentine's Day). When I witnessed the thoughtful gesture from my boys I was reminded of Scott's impact. These past few days have pushed me to reflect on this past year: who I was before Scott, what we were together and who I have become.

I have always had a thirst for adventure, but when I married Scott, that thirst got a shot of adrenaline. His trust in God and infectious curiosity for the unexplored took us many places in ministry and life...the BIG STUFF. However, it also showed up in little everyday ways. If there was a new restaurant, event, piece of technology, entertainment...he had to check it out and I came along willingly. He may have liked it...or not...but had to see for himself. He didn't want to rely on others' opinions. He needed first-hand knowledge, so needless to say, we had up-close and personal experiences with every coffee shop or donut establishment in Knoxville. I loved it when he would say, "Wanna go check it out?" I never declined his invitation for adventure, no matter how small.

This past year I have found myself home a lot more. I chalk it up to not having high school sporting events and church commitments every night of the week or just being exhausted by my responsibilities and emotions...maybe both. I see how easy it would be to lose my sense of adventure because I don't have my fellow explorer tempting me with his new found research. I love this side of me that he enhanced and I don't want to neglect it. So...on the 19th I will go somewhere I have never gone, eat something I have never tried and celebrate Scott for the impact he had on not just so many others...but ME.

Even though we had many adventures together, there were the few we experienced separately - the mission trips, family trips or events that called for one of us to go and the other stay home with the boys. We would always return to each other and share hours of conversation about our trips. These conversations would always end with..."We have to go back there together," or "I can't wait to show you," or "I wish you could have seen...you would have loved it." Even though life did not always allow it, we wanted to share everything.

My plan from this point forward is to take a moment on all future adventures to smile and say…"Scott, are you seeing this?" Thank you God for using people in our lives to show us MORE.

For nothing is impossible with God.

Luke 1:37

Now to him who is able to do IMMEASURABLY MORE than all we ask or imagine, according to his power that is at work within us.

Ephesians 3:20

I thank my God every time I remember you…

Philippians 1:3

So this week, embrace the intriguing unknown that God may be calling you to. No matter how small or scary it may be, know that our God is able to do IMMEASURABLY MORE… trust HIS MORE.

As always…I love you dearly and thank you for being a part of my MORE.

Saturday, February 23, 2019

As my finger touched the word "status" on my page this morning, it felt surreal. This will be the 53rd post (with one or two extras) chronicling my life since Scott's death. These Saturday morning posts have been a picture of my journey. The thing about pictures and words is they require interpretation. As each of you read my post, you take from it the elements that speak to you. It may be something you relate to in its exact form or a lesson that can be used for another circumstance you are walking through. You see it as it calls to you personally. The Bible and its God-ordained words have been yet another example of this interpretation for me this year. When it talks of being broken, humbled, thankful, trusting...new and personal meaning is attached to it.

I shared two weeks ago of my anxiety building up to the anniversary of Scott's death. It's weird to say "anniversary" because that word has always had such a positive feel to it. In its noun form, Webster's calls it "a yearly recurrence of the date of a past event." But in the adjective form it says, "returning or recurring each year." So, if this date is going to RETURN each year...what do I want to remember about February 19th? This question hung in my thoughts this week.

On the 19th, the boys and I went to Bald River Falls, Indian Boundary Lake and hiked to the top of Huckleberry Bald. It was good just to move, be active and see beautiful things. As we stood on top of the bald with its 360 degree view, it began to snow. It felt so good to let it hit my face as we hiked down. God once again reminded me that I would continue to experience beautiful things on my journey. Later that evening we watched old home videos. It was so good to remember. The very thing I was afraid of these past two weeks...REMEMBERING! When night came it was quiet and I was alone. I thanked God for ALL the memories...even the painful ones. I realized that so many painful moments were securely attached to beautiful ones. The sweet faces of so many of you who came to the hospital to check on us and say goodbye to Scott will be attached to my memory of his body lying in that bed. I remember those of you who were not afraid to love us in our darkest moments. I remember those who traveled a great distance to be here for Scott's funeral. I remember the hundreds of messages I received, in numerous forms, in the weeks after his passing...showing his vast impact. These memories will be attached to my pain from that week. The overwhelming generosity of time and resources given to me will be attached to my paralyzing grief during those first days. My every need was met above and beyond. I want you to know I remember everything - every face, card, message, meal, hug and tear. It was the Body of Christ at its finest moment for me. There is so much beauty in the marriage of pain and love. We have the capacity to hurt deeply only because it matches our capacity to love deeply.

The day after this anniversary, God reminded me that one year later...I am not forgotten. The messages, hugs, flowers, milkshakes and gifts came pouring in this week just as they did a year ago. He reassured me that my grief may look different this year, but His presence in the midst of my journey will not change.

I am holding tightly to a handful of words right now: Journey...Path...Direction...Joy...Trust...Thankfulness. Some of these words are the same ones I clutched tightly to this time last year, but they are taking on a new interpretation.

Therefore, since we are surrounded by such a GREAT CLOUD OF WITNESSES let us throw off everything

that hinders, and the sin that so easily entangles, and let
us RUN with perseverance the race MARKED OUT
FOR US. Let us fix our eyes on Jesus, the author and
perfecter of our faith, who for the JOY SET BEFORE
HIM endured the cross, scorning its shame, and sat
down at the right hand of the throne of God.

Hebrews 12:1-2

Here is my personal interpretation of this verse…right now…
based on my experiences this year.

I am swollen with gratefulness for YOU...my "GREAT
CLOUD OF WITNESSES."

I have been walking my "path, journey, direction," but it is now
time to "RUN" the race "MARKED OUT FOR" me.

My focus will be "THE JOY SET BEFORE" me.

I will close this year of posts saying that I have tried to
be honest, raw and encouraging. I entered into every post
with humble curiosity, not knowing what I should say (no
scripted thoughts). Many times the words my finger typed on
my phone were not what I would have said that week, but
what God wanted shared. I have remained committed to my
promise...***"Your Words, Not Mine."*** I do not know if I will
sit in this same spot, on the left side of my couch, with feet
tucked under me and coffee on the table beside me to post next
Saturday morning. I do know that there will be more to share...
because I have more to my story.

My prayer for all of you is that you share your story, with
all its victories and vulnerable moments. Just like my posts...use
your quotation marks, all caps, and dot-dot-dots…to emphasize

what God is doing in you. Take time for solitude to sit in God's presence. If you don't, you may miss what he wants to show you.

Be still, and know that I am God…
Psalms 46:10

I LOVE YOU with all the capacity given me to LOVE.

About the Author

Penny Sparks is wife and widow, mother to three sons and intentional follower of Christ, who unexpectedly found herself a widow after 26 years of marriage. Scott was a healthy fifty-one year old who came home from a high school basketball game with flu symptoms. Thirteen days later, he was gone. When Scott died, Penny did not just lose her husband, she lost her soulmate and partner in ministry. In honor of her late husband and love of her life, she is committed to sharing her story.